W9-CRN-038

Culture and Modern Life

David Matsumoto

San Francisco State University

Brooks/Cole Publishing Company

I(T)P®An International Thomson Publishing Company

Pacific Grove • Albany • Belmont • Bonn • Boston • Cincinnati
Detroit • Johannesburg • London • Madrid • Melbourne • Mexico City
New York • Paris • Singapore • Tokyo • Toronto • Washington

For Sayaka

Sponsoring Editor: *Marianne Taflinger*
Editorial Associate: *Scott Brearton*
Production Editor: *Ellen Brownstein*
Production Service: *Scratchgravel Publishing Services*
Marketing Team: *Lauren Harp and Deborah Petit*

Manuscript Editor: *Anne Draus*
Permissions Editor: *Carline Haga*
Cover Design: *E. Kelly Shoemaker*
Typesetting: *Scratchgravel Publishing Services*
Printing and Binding: *Edwards Brothers, Inc., Ann Arbor, MI*

For more information, contact:

BROOKS/COLE PUBLISHING COMPANY
511 Forest Lodge Road
Pacific Grove, CA 93950
USA

International Thomson Publishing Europe
Berkshire House 168-173
High Holborn
London WC1V 7AA
England

Thomas Nelson Australia
102 Dodds Street
South Melbourne, 3205
Victoria, Australia

Nelson Canada
1120 Birchmount Road
Scarborough, Ontario
Canada M1K 5G4

International Thomson Editores
Seneca 53, Col. Polanco
México, D. F., México
C. P. 11560

International Thomson Publishing GmbH
Königswinterer Strasse 418
53227 Bonn
Germany

International Thomson Publishing Asia
221 Henderson Road
#05-10 Henderson Building
Singapore 0315

International Thomson Publishing Japan
Hirakawacho Kyowa Building, 3F
2-2-1 Hirakawacho
Chiyoda-ku, Tokyo 102
Japan

Printed in the United States of America

10   9   8   7   6   5   4   3   2   1

Library of Congress Cataloging-in-Publication Data
Matsumoto, David Ricky.
   Culture and modern life / David Matsumoto.
     p.   cm.
   Includes bibliographical references and index.
   ISBN 0-534-49688-1 (pbk.)
   1. Ethnopsychology.   2. Social psychology.   3. Adjustment
(Psychology)   I. Title.
IN PROCESS
155.8'2—dc20
                              9630685
                                CIP

Contents

8 *Conclusion*   *112*

References   *119*

Index   *128*

Preface

This book is intended for use as a supplemental textbook in courses on psychological adjustment. By reviewing cross-cultural research literature in six popular areas of psychology, this text challenges much of the knowledge that is typically presented in larger, more traditional psychology of adjustment texts and courses. As a supplement, this text presents a much more detailed discussion of the issues than would be possible if integrated in the body of a main text, which often makes the material appear superficial or tokenistic. In challenging the traditional knowledge, the overall goals of the book are to expose students in adjustment courses to psychology from around the world, to improve their critical thinking skills, and to provide options from which they can choose the perspective on psychology and human behavior that is right for them in their own efforts to improve their lives.

In the following sections I describe in more detail the rationale for this book as well as its structure and its major themes.

The Purpose of This Book

Psychology from a Limited Perspective

In psychological adjustment classes across the United States today, we try to present to students many of the "truths" that have been gathered through scientific research in psychology over the years. Armed with a compilation of those facts (the textbook) and associated resources (videos, computer disks, instructor's manual, and so on), psychology marches on in teaching students what we know about human behavior.

For many students, much of the information presented in mainstream texts strikes a familiar chord; thus, the nature of the truth that is presented is validated for these students. For many other students, however, much of that same "truth" is just too "foreign." Many leave their classes frustrated or confused, wondering about the relevance to their lives of what they have learned. For them, the truth that was presented is not validated. Many teachers may also feel the same way.

To understand the basis of these frustrations, we need to examine how the truths were produced in the first place. Most, if not all, of the information presented in mainstream texts is based on findings from research. Until recently, most of the research conducted in psychology was based on only a single type of person—middle-class Americans of European descent enrolled in introductory psychology classes in American universities, participating in research to fulfill class requirements.

Although there is nothing wrong with such research, and thus its findings, there are limitations to the types of knowledge and information that can be gathered this way. For one thing, we wouldn't know whether what we found to be true for this group of people would apply to people of other racial, cultural, or ethnic backgrounds. Do people of *all* backgrounds learn in the same way? Develop in the same way? Express emotions in the same way? React to different psychotherapies in the same way? Such questions suggest that principles can be limited.

Many factors may have contributed to our previous lack of concern about these potential limitations. One of those is that American psychology has been quite ethnocentric and has fostered, to a large degree, an ignorance of the psychologies of other countries and cultures. Another reason has to do with the funds available for research, which ultimately influence the truths that are produced; for many years, funding agencies were not very concerned with cross-cultural or subcultural research. Yet a third reason is the lack of subjects of different racial, ethnic, and cultural backgrounds; thus, it was more difficult than it is today to study differences even if the researchers wanted to. A fourth reason has to do with the politics of uncovering cultural differences and the interpretation of values that are often associated. Finally, a fifth reason for a lack of knowledge and awareness about ethnic and cultural differences involves the lack of ethnic and cultural diversity among the researchers themselves.

Unfortunately, by presenting psychological principles from this limited perspective, such textbooks really have done no justice to one of the greatest attributes of people—the individual and collective diversity in thought, feeling, and behavior. This diversity is exactly what psychology is supposed to understand.

Why This Book?

We need to ask some very basic, yet extremely important, questions about the nature of the knowledge and information typically taught and learned in psychology classes across America today. These questions concern such topics as the limitations of the information traditionally presented in mainstream textbooks and the degree to which this information is applicable to people of different ethnic, racial, or cultural backgrounds. Findings from cross-cultural research can inform us about how studies of people of different cultures, both inside and outside the United States, challenge the traditional information. Then, to the extent that we can find evidence to suggest that the "traditional" information is limited, we need to revise our understanding of that information.

This book is one of our first serious attempts to answer these important questions facing teachers and students of psychological adjustment. Indeed, ethnic and cultural diversity has emerged as one of the hottest topics in psychology today. This book is a must for gaining some perspective on the issue of human diversity in the study of psychology.

How Is This Book Organized?

Topics Selected and Guiding Themes

This book is not intended to replace your main textbook. It does not provide a comprehensive review or presentation of the traditional material typically covered. Instead, this book *supplements* psychology textbooks by *re*-presenting some of the same material, but with a cross-cultural focus. Material was taken from two of my previously published books—*People: Psychology from a Cultural Perspective* and *Culture and Psychology*. The former is a supplemental text for introductory psychology courses; the latter is designed for use in cross-cultural psychology courses.

What material have I chosen to re-present? This was a difficult decision, because many people believe that students should learn *every* major topic and subfield in psychology from a cross-cultural perspective. However, that is just not realistic. Psychology courses are already pressed for time without rehashing every single topic from a different viewpoint. Thus, I chose topics for this book that are typically covered in adjustment textbooks, have special relevance to issues of adjustment, and have sufficient cross-cultural work to present something meaningful. I took special care in ensuring that the topic coverage matched that of the widely used adjustment text by Wayne Weiten and Margaret Lloyd, *Psychology and Modern Life*. Instructors using this text, and others, should be pleased with the topic coverage.

Several questions served as guiding themes in writing each of the chapters in this book. These themes include the following:

1. What is "typically" presented on this topic in mainstream texts?

2. What are the limitations in this knowledge due to the cultural composition of the samples studied in the research that forms the basis of this knowledge? To what degree is this knowledge generalizable to people of other cultural backgrounds?

3. How do findings from cross-cultural research challenge traditional knowledge?

4. Given differences in knowledge from cross-cultural research, how can we, or should we, think about this topic?

In a supplemental text it is impossible to review all the cross-cultural literature on a topic or to ensure adequate representation of a variety of cultures in the presentation. Instead, we have selected studies that are intended to raise questions about the traditional knowledge and to serve as examples of how that knowledge may be culture bound.

Overall Book Goals

This book seeks to raise questions about traditional, mainstream knowledge, to know whether what is taught is applicable to people of *all* cultural backgrounds. It looks for answers to these questions in the cross-cultural literature. If the research suggests that people are different from what is typically presented, I try to find ways of understanding those differences that are better than those available today.

I offer this book as a way to seek alternatives to the material typically presented in psychology. By offering these alternatives, I hope that students will be able to choose a perspective of psychology and human behavior that is right for them. Also, I hope that they will be able to recognize, understand, and most important, appreciate the psychology of people of diverse backgrounds, some of which will be very, very different from their own.

Acknowledgments

This book is the product of a collaborative effort by many friends and colleagues. I am in debt to many of them for helping me, directly and indirectly, in making this book and its predecessors reality.

Over the years, my research laboratory at San Francisco State University, and earlier at the Wright Institute and the University of California,

Berkeley, has benefited from the participation of many undergraduate and graduate research assistants. Although there are too many of them to name specifically, I would like to single out the assistants who helped compile much of the information used in my previous books, on which this book is based. Without the help of Michelle Weissman, Michael Biehl, Fazilet Kasri, and Sachiko Takeuchi, this book would never have been completed. They are all fine researchers in their own right, and I consider them my close friends.

The material in Chapters 2 and 7 were taken mainly from my book *People: Psychology from a Cultural Perspective*. Contributions to these chapters were made by author collaborators Dawn Terrell, Shinobu Kitayama, and Hazel Markus. I am indebted to them for the fine work they did on that project, which enabled me to complete this project.

I am grateful to Marianne Taflinger, my editor at Brooks/Cole Publishing Company, for having the courage and vision to engage in the publication of my previous works, which led to this one. Marianne has always been very supportive of many efforts to bring culture into the teaching of psychology. I also extend my gratitude to Ellen Brownstein, Kelly Shoemaker, and Scott Brearton at Brooks Cole and to Anne and Greg Draus at Scratchgravel.

I am thankful to Wayne Weiten for his desire to have my work coupled with his. His comments about this book have guided how I approached the compilation and drafting of the material. I am humbled and honored to have worked with him on this project.

Finally, I thank all of my students, past, present, and future, for all they have taught me about psychology, culture, and modern life. They are, indeed, the wind beneath my wings.

David Matsumoto

About the Author

David Matsumoto is a Professor of Psychology and Director of the Inter-cultural and Emotion Research Laboratory at San Francisco State University. He earned his B.A. from the University of Michigan and his M.A. and Ph.D from the University of California, Berkeley. He has studied emotion, human interaction, and culture for over 15 years and is a recognized expert in this field. He is the author of over 90 works on culture and emotion, including original research articles, paper presentations, books, chapters in books, videos, and assessment instruments. He has been invited to address professional and scientific groups in the United States and abroad, including the Russian Academy of Sciences in Moscow. He also serves as an intercultural consultant to various domestic and international businesses.

Dr. Matsumoto brings his expertise in intercultural relations to the arena of the Olympic sport of judo. He currently serves as the Chairman of National Coaching and Training and the National Coaching Staff for United States Judo, Inc., the national governing body of judo in the United States. He was the designated team leader for the judo team representing the United States at the 1995 World Championships in Chiba, Japan, and in the 1996 Summer Olympic Games in Atlanta, Georgia.

Related Titles by David Matsumoto

Culture and Psychology
People: Psychology from a Cultural Perspective
Cultural Influences on Methods and Statistics
A World of Diversity video with student workbook and facilitator's guide

Introduction

Applying the principles of psychology to everyday life is not an easy task. Certainly, there are many principles about human behavior that psychologists have discovered over the years. Most, if not all, of these principles about behavior have come from systematic and in-depth studies conducted with a variety of research methods and traditions (qualitative and quantitative methods, single-case and sampling methods, and so on). Many of these principles serve as the large foundation of fundamental knowledge in psychology and are presented to you in psychology textbooks at all levels.

Despite the fact that psychologists have amassed a considerable wealth of knowledge about people, there are still many times when knowledge does not match reality. Principles are basically broad guidelines about human behavior, generalizations of research findings accumulated over the years. As such, there are bound to be many individual differences in relation to these principles. Some people may behave exactly as they "should" according to principle, whereas others may behave "just about" the way the principles suggest, with minor differences. Still other people may behave entirely differently. All people are different, and these differences contribute to differences in the accuracy of these principles to characterize human behavior well.

Not only are people different, but so too are the contexts and situations within which they live and operate. These contextual, situational, social, and cultural differences also contribute to differences in the accuracy of the psychological principles we have to adequately describe human behavior.

To be sure, differences among people, context, or culture do not necessarily lead to fundamental differences in psychological functioning.

Indeed, studies across cultures and contexts have shown that there are important similarities among people as well. It is just as important to understand similarities as it is to understand differences.

This book examines how culture influences our knowledge about basic psychological processes. Culture is just one of many contexts that can produce similarities as well as differences in psychological functioning. Thus, it follows that the psychological principles we derive about people may be consistent or discrepant across cultures. To the extent that differences do exist, it is important for all of us to appreciate how cultural factors moderate our psychological processes. In gaining such appreciation, we can learn how our own viewpoint, developed within our own cultural framework, can distort our interpretation of others' behaviors. At the same time, we need to know what kinds of cross-cultural similarities exist in psychological principles and basic processes. Knowledge about these similarities as well should help us in our endeavors to apply these principles to improve our lives.

The branch of psychology that allows for these types of examinations is called cross-cultural psychology. In order to help achieve our goal of uncovering cross-cultural similarities and differences in principles and processes through an examination of cross-cultural research, we begin here with an understanding of the role of cross-cultural psychology within the greater field of psychology and discuss the nature of exactly how facts become principles.

The Nature of Knowledge in Psychology

One of the most important goals of the field of psychology is to understand human behavior. In this sense, psychology is similar to philosophy, which also attempts to understand people. Yet psychologists are different from philosophers in the way they approach the problem. Psychology relies heavily on scientific *research* about people to generate what knowledge we have about how and why people behave. Typically, before we accept something as a "truth" in psychology (many call these truths "principles"), we have to be assured that the research that produced that truth met some minimal standards for scientific rigor. Thus, the **psychological truth** born from the research could be only that and nothing else.

It follows, then, that what we know as truths in psychology are heavily dependent on how the research that produced those truths was conducted. Because of the nature of research, *all* studies in psychology are conducted under some conditions, within certain parameters and limitations. Thus, to a large extent, all the knowledge generated by psychological research is bounded by parameters and limitations.

What are some of these parameters? Well, in psychological research, there are many parameters and thus limitations. Some have to do with the nature of the *task* that is given to the participants. These might include a questionnaire, a problem to solve, or viewing stimuli in a tachistoscope. Some parameters have to do with the *environment* or *setting* in which the study is conducted. These might include the location of the study (laboratory room, classroom, home), the time of day, the color of the surroundings, and the like. Finally, some parameters have to do with the nature of the *participants* in the research. Typically, these include the participants' gender, race or ethnicity, socioeconomic status, culture, religious affiliation, and so forth.

All studies in psychology are conducted within a set of specific parameters. For example, a study of facial expressions may involve *white, middle-class males* and *females* viewing a set of *30* different facial expressions in a *laboratory experiment room* and making a *free-response* judgment of what emotion they perceive in the expressions. Whatever data we obtained from this particular study would constitute some knowledge ("facts"), and this knowledge would be bounded by the specific parameters within which the study was conducted.

Of course, we never know whether or not the facts gathered from one study can be applicable to more people than were originally involved in the study. Luckily, most of the material that is typically presented in textbooks is not knowledge that was generated from a single study under its specific parameters. Indeed, the knowledge generated from single studies is rather limited because it was generated only once, under a set of specific parameters. Rather, the material that is presented in textbooks is that which has usually been shown in more than one study—perhaps in two, three, or more. Thus, that knowledge is generally regarded as a "truth" or "principle" in psychology. By relying on such a process of research and repeated consistent findings (called *replication*), psychologists can generally accept as "truth" knowledge that weathers the test of time and, more concretely, multiple experiments. If these studies involved people of different races and socioeconomic backgrounds, presented with different numbers and types of stimuli, in different laboratory or natural settings, and we *still* obtained the same findings, we would be fairly well convinced that the knowledge we have obtained is true for all people in multiple contexts.

What Is Cross-Cultural Psychology, and How Does It Impact on Psychological Truths?

Cross-cultural psychology is a branch of psychology that is primarily concerned with testing possible limitations to knowledge by studying people of different cultures. In its strictest sense, **cross-cultural research**

simply involves the inclusion of participants from different cultural backgrounds and the testing of possible differences among these participants. In its broadest sense, however, cross-cultural psychology is concerned with understanding truth and psychological principles as either universal (that is, true for all people of all cultures) or culture-specific (true for some people of some cultures).

Cross-cultural psychology is not topic-specific. That is, cross-cultural psychologists are interested in a broad range of phenomena related to human behavior, from perception to language, child-rearing to psychopathology. What delineates cross-cultural psychology from "traditional" or "mainstream" psychology, therefore, is not the phenomenon of interest. Rather, it is the testing of limitations to knowledge by examining whether that knowledge is applicable or obtainable in people of different cultural backgrounds. Given this definition of cross-cultural psychology, psychologists can apply cross-cultural techniques in testing the universality or cultural specificity of any and all aspects of human behavior.

Although research in cross-cultural psychology has existed for many years, it has gained in popularity over the past few years. Because of its relative youth in mainstream, academic psychology, there is a relative lack of textbooks that specifically address cross-cultural issues regarding psychological adjustment. The purpose of this book is to provide such a resource. I have chosen some topics in psychology that are very well established in cross-cultural research and that are also typically covered in mainstream psychological adjustment textbooks and courses. In each, I will discuss how cross-cultural research has tested some of the limitations to knowledge generated in single-culture research. My goals, which I will discuss in greater detail at the end of this chapter, are simply to introduce you to this major line of inquiry in psychology and to offer you alternatives to what is typically presented as psychological "truth." The underlying premise to all of this is that understanding the constraints and boundaries of cultural similarities and differences on psychological principles helps us gain more accurate information about those principles which is, in turn, of greater value to you in everyday life

Before proceeding further, however, it is important to deal with what we mean when we use the word *culture*.

A Definition of Culture

Despite the fact that most of us probably feel that we know what culture is, culture is a rather difficult concept to define formally. Scholars such as Margaret Mead, Ruth Benedict, Geert Hofstede, and others have offered a number of interesting definitions of culture. For our purposes, we define **culture** as the set of attitudes, values, beliefs, and behaviors shared by a group of people, communicated from one generation to the next via language or some other means of communication (Barnouw, 1985).

This definition of culture is "fuzzy." That is, there are necessarily no hard and fast rules of how to determine what a culture is or who belongs to that culture. In this sense, culture is a sociopsychological construct, a sharing across people of psychological phenomena such as values, attitudes, beliefs, and behaviors. Members of the same culture share these psychological phenomena. Members of different cultures do not.

Culture is not necessarily rooted in biology. That is, culture is not race. Two people of the same race can either share the same values and behaviors—that is, culture—or they can be very disparate in their cultural makeups. Now, it is true that people of the same racial heritage *in general* may share the same socialization processes and may be *enculturated* in similar ways. Thus, we may speak of a Hispanic culture or an African-American culture or an Asian culture. But, it is also true that there need not be a one-to-one correspondence between race and culture. Just because one is born a certain race does not necessarily mean that one adopts the culture that is stereotypic of that race.

Culture is also not nationality. Just because a person is from France, for example, does not necessarily mean that he or she will act in accordance with what one would consider the dominant French culture or with stereotypes of French people. Just as culture does not necessarily conform to race or racial stereotypes, culture also does not necessarily conform to nationality or citizenship. In fact, there is ample and growing evidence to suggest that a small but substantial portion of the population of many different countries do not "match" the dominant cultural stereotype of their country (Triandis, 1992).

In this sense, culture is as much an individual, psychological construct as it is a macro, social construct. That is, to some extent, culture exists in each and every one of us individually as much as it exists as a global, social construct. Individual differences in culture can be observed among people in the degree to which they adopt and engage in the attitudes, values, beliefs, and behaviors that, by consensus, constitute their culture. If you act in accordance with certain shared values or behaviors, then that culture resides in you; if you do not share those values or behaviors, then you do not share that culture.

Etics, Emics, Ethnocentrism, and Stereotypes

One of the major ways of conceptualizing principles in cross-cultural psychology is through the use of the terms *etics* and *emics*. These terms are very related to our previous discussion concerning universality or cultural specificity of knowledge and truths. An **etic** refers to findings that appear to be consistent across different cultures; that is, an etic refers to a universal truth or principle. An **emic**, in contrast, refers to findings that appear to be different across cultures; an emic, therefore, refers to truths that are culture-specific.

The concepts of emics and etics are powerful because of their implications about what we may know as truth. If we know something about human behavior and we regard it as a truth, *and* it is an etic (that is, universal), then the truth as we know it is truth for all, regardless of culture. If that something we know about human behavior and regard as truth, however, is an emic (that is, culture-specific), then what we regard as truth is not necessarily what someone from another culture regards as truth. In fact, they may be quite different! Truth, in this sense, is relative, not absolute. This type of definition of truth with regard to emics and etics should force us all to consider whether what we believe is true or not.

There are many examples of both emics and etics in cross-cultural psychology. Indeed, it may be fair to say that one of the major goals of cross-cultural psychology as a discipline is to uncover exactly which aspects of human behavior are emics and which are etics. One of the major goals in each of the subsequent chapters in this book is to present examples of emics and etics that have been generated by cross-cultural research.

Most cross-cultural psychologists would agree that there are many emics. People of different cultures find many different ways of living and interacting with one another. These cultural differences are due to many factors, such as the availability of resources, population density within the culture, physical and geographic limitations, and the like. Thus, it is not surprising that each culture evolves in its own distinct way to "manage" human behaviors in the most efficient and appropriate fashion to ensure successful survival. To the extent that each culture must meet different needs in the environment, each culture will develop differences in the ways in which it impacts on the people within it.

The existence of many emics, or cultural differences, per se is not problematic in and of itself. There is potential for problems, however, when one attempts to *interpret* the reasons underlying or producing those differences. Because we all exist in our own cultures with our own cultural backgrounds, we tend to see things through that background. That is, culture acts as a filter, not only when perceiving things, but also when thinking about and interpreting events. We may interpret someone else's behavior from our own cultural background and come to some conclusion about that behavior based on our own beliefs of culture and behavior. Our interpretation may be wrong, however, if the behavior that we are judging originates from a different cultural orientation than our own. In some cases (more than we all think!), we may be way off in our interpretation of other people's behavior.

For example, suppose you are having a conversation with a person from a culture different from yours. While you are talking to this person, you notice that she does not really make eye contact with you when she speaks. Also, she does not really look at you when you speak. On the few occasions when her eyes look your way, she quickly averts her gaze if your eyes meet. From your cultural background, you may interpret that she does not feel very positive about you or your interaction. You may even feel put off and reject any attempts at future interaction. You may not feel trusting or close to her. But she may come from a culture where direct gazing is discouraged or is even a sign of arrogance or slight. She may actually be avoiding eye contact not because of any negative feelings, but because of deference and politeness to you! Of course, these potential problems have real and practical implications in everyday life. Think about this scenario occurring in a job interview, in a teaching/learning situation at an elementary school, during a business negotiation, or even in a visit with your therapist! Thus, while the outward behavioral manifestation may be emic or culture-specific, the underlying intention (for example, to get along) may be etic or cross-cultural. In this fashion, human behaviors can represent both etic (underlying intentions) and emic (outward behaviors) roots. Problems often occur when we interpret emics in terms of our own cultural meanings.

Sometimes we cannot separate ourselves from our own cultural backgrounds and biases to understand the behaviors of others. This type of resistance forms the basis of what is known as **ethnocentrism**—the viewing and interpretation of the behavior of others through one's own cultural filters. All people—students and faculty, laypersons and researchers alike—need to be aware of these biases and tendencies in understanding the behaviors of others of different cultural backgrounds.

Ethnocentrism is closely related to another important topic—stereotypes. **Stereotypes** are fixed attitudes, beliefs, or opinions about people who belong to cultures other than one's own. They may be born of fact. Often, however, stereotypes are combinations of fact and fiction about people from a certain cultural group. Stereotypes may be handy in giving people some kind of basis in judging, evaluating, and interacting with people of other cultures. They can be very dangerous and damaging, however, when people adhere to them inflexibly and apply the stereotypes to all people of that cultural background without recognizing the possible false bases of the stereotype as well as individual differences within that culture.

We often find that we are different from people of other cultures, either through research or through our everyday interactions and experiences. Our discovery of these differences can have severe and serious negative consequences. The potential for misuse occurs when *values* such as good/bad, right/wrong, superior/inferior are attached to the behaviors of others that are different from one's own culture.

Emics, etics, ethnocentrism, and stereotypes are all important concepts to learn about and remember. As we progress through our studies of cultural similarities and differences, it is important to have some idea of what the potential pitfalls may be. Needless to say, making value statements and maintaining an ethnocentric attitude are not conducive to healthy psychological adjustment.

The Need for Incorporating Cross-Cultural Issues in Learning about Mainstream Psychology

There is a lot of information in the field of psychology that is considered truth. Regardless, it is vitally important now to incorporate cross-cultural issues into our knowledge of psychology for at least two reasons. The first has to do with what is known as "scientific philosophy." This refers to what we have been discussing all along in this chapter—the need to evaluate our truths in terms of the parameters within which those truths were obtained. More simply put, we need to examine whether the information we have learned (or will learn in the future) is applicable to *all* people of *all* cultures (that is, it is an etic), or whether it is applicable to *some* people of *some* cultures (in which case, it is an emic). Or more aptly, we need to learn to examine how behaviors may be an emic and an etic at the same time. Scientific philosophy refers to the notion that we have a duty, an obligation, to ask these questions about the scientific process and about the nature of the truths we have learned, or will learn, in psychology.

The second reason that it is important to incorporate cross-cultural issues in psychology is much more practical. Psychology involves the study of human behavior to improve our understanding of ourselves and others. One of the goals of this endeavor is to help us in our real-life, everyday interactions and dealings with others. As we have more frequent contact with people of different cultural backgrounds, it becomes increasingly imperative that we learn about emics and etics in our truths—that is, in the beliefs we hold about people and the way they are. To be ignorant of such emics and etics would make us guilty of ethnocentrism and would hamper our everyday dealings with others.

In order to gain a better appreciation of psychological principles that can help in everyday life, it is important to gain a better appreciation of the basic processes of research that contributed to those principles. Thus, many textbooks on adjustment include a discussion about research fundamentals. Likewise, in order to gain a better appreciation of the knowledge gathered from cross-cultural psychology, it is best to have some basic knowledge about the fundamentals of cross-cultural research. The next section presents some issues that are unique to cross-cultural research.

Some Special Issues Concerning Cross-Cultural Research Methodology

As we turn to the cross-cultural literature for knowledge about the boundaries of psychological truths, it is important to discuss some issues that are especially relevant to the conduct of cross-cultural research. These issues include the operational definitions of culture used in the studies, sampling, sample equivalence, the formulation of research questions, and the interpretation of data, language, and response sets. Most of these issues, with the possible exception of language, are just as salient and important to mainstream psychological research. We focus our discussion here, however, on their relevance to cross-cultural research.

Operational Definitions of Culture

As we discussed earlier, most cross-cultural psychologists would agree that culture is the shared conglomeration of attitudes, values, behaviors, and beliefs, communicated from one generation to the next through language. This definition of culture is psychological, not biological. Despite this definition of culture, cross-cultural researchers have lacked an adequate way of measuring the "sharing" of psychological characteristics in their research. Instead, they have relied on aspects of people that are easier to measure—typically, race (such as European American, Chinese, Mexican, African American) and nationality (American, Japanese, German, Brazilian, and so on). But, as we discussed earlier in this chapter, culture is not necessarily either race or nationality. It is, indeed, a truly sociopsychological construct.

Without a way to measure culture on the sociopsychological level, in accordance with our definition of culture, researchers have had to "trade off" the ability to really study cross-cultural differences. Indeed, most, if not all, of the studies conducted to date, and presented in this book, have measured culture by either race or nationality. Still, we cannot categorically dismiss these studies or their findings. They do provide valuable information about possible cultural differences and limitations to what we know and regard as truth from research in mainstream psychology. Thus, it is still important for us to consider these studies. But we must consider them with caution concerning the discrepancy between our definition of culture and that definition of culture used in the research.

Sampling

In the simplest cross-cultural research design, a researcher obtains a sample of people in one culture, obtains data from them, and compares those data to other data or known values. Let's say, for example, that a researcher obtained a sample of 50 Americans as part of a cross-cultural study. Are the 50 Americans adequate representatives of the American culture? If they were recruited from Beverly Hills in California, would that be the same as recruiting 50 participants from the Bronx in New York? From Wichita, Kansas? If the 50 participants were all of European descent, would they be an "adequate" sample? If not, what percentage of people of different racial and ethnic backgrounds would the researcher need to be satisfied (given that it is too difficult to measure "true" culture)? If the sample required 25% to be of African descent, could *any* African American be recruited to make 25%? What criteria would be used to decide whether the sample of 50 people were adequate representatives of the American culture? What is the definition of the "American" culture, anyway?

These are not easy questions to deal with, and they pertain to any sample of participants in *any* culture. Cross-cultural researchers need to pay particular attention to issues of sampling in the conduct of their research. Aside from being able (or unable) to measure culture on a psychological level, cross-cultural researchers need to ensure that the participants in their studies are adequate representatives of their culture, whatever it is, if the researcher wants to draw conclusions about cultural differences from those samples.

Sample Equivalence

Just obtaining samples that are adequate representatives of their culture is not sufficient to conducting valid cross-cultural research. Researchers need to make sure that the samples they compare are somehow equivalent on noncultural, demographic variables. Without ascertaining similarity in demographic characteristics, there is no rational basis to attribute group differences to culture as opposed to these other demographics. The same findings may be obtained if groups were differentiated according to those demographics (for example, educational background, socioeconomic status). Cross-cultural researchers need to establish some basis of equivalence between their samples in order to make cultural comparisons meaningful.

Formulation of Research Questions and Interpretation of Data

The very questions researchers decide to study are culture bound. That is, the questions may be meaningful in one culture, but not necessarily so in another. Cultural differences found in studies where this disparity exists are confounded by it. That is, it is impossible to know whether researchers are finding a "true" cultural difference in response or merely differences due to meaning of the questions being asked.

In addition to the disparity of culture-bound questions, we also have to consider the interpretation of the cross-cultural data obtained. The researchers who are conducting the study are often from a cultural background that is different from that of the subjects in the study. The researchers will inevitably interpret the data they obtain (whether from questionnaires, responses to a task, or whatever) through their own cultural filters. Their interpretation of the data the subjects produce may not have anything to do with what the subjects actually intended in producing the data. That is, the subjects are operating out of their own cultural background, which may be entirely different from that of the researchers. The interpretation of data obtained in cross-cultural research, therefore, is particularly tricky.

Language and Translation Issues

All cross-cultural research cannot be conducted in English. If you were to compare the questionnaire responses of an American sample to those from Beijing, you would need to have both an English and a Chinese version of the questionnaire. How are we to know that the questionnaires themselves are equivalent? Cross-cultural researchers frequently use a **back-translation** procedure to ensure some type of equivalence in their research protocols. This procedure involves taking the protocol in one language, translating it to the other, and having someone else translate it back to the original. If the back-translated version is the same as the original, then some type of equivalence exists. If it is not, the procedure is repeated until the back-translated version is exactly the same as the original.

Still, even if the *words* being used in the two languages are the same, how do we know that exactly the same meanings, with the same nuances, are attributed to those words in the two cultures? Any differences that we find between the cultures may be due to linguistic or semantic differences in the research protocols used in conducting the study. Cross-cultural researchers need to deal with these issues of language equivalence, so that these issues are not confused with any cultural differences they want to test.

Response Sets

Response sets refer to a cultural tendency to respond a certain way on tests or response scales that is reflective more of the cultural tendency than of the meaning of the actual scale. For example, participants in the United States and Hong Kong may be asked to judge the intensity of a certain stimulus, using a 7-point scale. When examining the data, the researcher may find that the Americans generally scored around 6 or 7, whereas the people from Hong Kong generally scored around 4 or 5. The researcher may then interpret that the Americans perceived more intensity in the stimulus than did the people from Hong Kong.

But what if the people from Hong Kong actually rate *everything* lower than the Americans do, not just that stimulus? What if they actually perceive a considerable amount of intensity in the stimulus but have a cultural tendency to use the lower part of the scale? This is not as far-fetched as it may seem. Some cultures, for example, encourage their members not to "stick out." Other cultures encourage their members to be unique and very individual. These types of cultural differences may result in different uses of response alternatives on questionnaires or in interviews. Some cultures may encourage extreme responses on a rating scale; others may discourage extreme responses and encourage responses around the "middle" of a scale. Subjects from two cultures may respond in entirely the same way on a questionnaire, except that the data may be located on different parts of the scale.

Themes and Goals of the Chapters

Cross-cultural research has its own special set of issues that must be addressed for the research to be valid. These and other issues have complicated cross-cultural studies in the past and have probably discouraged some researchers from conducting these types of studies. Recognizing and understanding these issues are important not only in conducting cross-cultural research but also as first steps in appreciating observed cultural differences. Yet, despite the difficulty of conducting cross-cultural research properly, many cross-cultural studies have important things to say about topics in psychology. Those studies that pass muster and that inform us about cultural diversity in human behavior form the basis of this book.

This book explores certain topics that are especially important to adjustment in modern life and that have a rich cross-cultural base. Each chapter in the book addresses a standard set of questions, including:

What is "typically" presented on this topic in traditional psychology?

What are the limitations in this knowledge due to the culture? To what degree is this knowledge generalizable to people of other cultural backgrounds?

How do findings from cross-cultural research challenge traditional knowledge?

Given differences in knowledge from cross-cultural research, how can we, or should we, think about this topic?

After all is said and done, what will you gain from this book? This book seeks to raise questions about traditional, mainstream findings, to ask whether what is told to you in such findings is applicable to people of *all* cultural backgrounds. This book challenges the traditional by seeking answers to these questions in the cross-cultural literature. If the research suggests that people are different from what is typically presented, then this book will help you find better ways of understanding those differences.

To challenge the traditional is not to disregard its importance, however. Doing so would be insensitive, and that should have no place in academic work. Instead, this book is a way to seek alternatives to the principles typically presented in psychology. Through these alternatives, you gain two important things that were previously unavailable to you.

1. By seeing alternative ways of observing and understanding people, you will have the ability to choose a viewpoint or perspective of psychology and human behavior that you believe is right for you.

2. By being exposed to these alternatives, you will be able to recognize, understand, and most important, appreciate the psychology of people of diverse backgrounds, some of which will be very, very different from your own.

In this book, there should be no right and wrong, no good and bad. We need to remember the dangers and potential pitfalls in making value judgments of good/bad or superior/inferior when cultural differences are observed. Indeed, there are just people—all different kinds of people.

Glossary

back-translation   A procedure used in cross-cultural research to ensure some type of equivalence in research protocols. This procedure involves taking the protocol in one language, translating it to the other, and having someone else translate it back to the original. If the back-translated version is the same as the original, then some type of equivalence exists. If it is not, the procedure is repeated until the back-translated version is exactly the same as the original.

cross-cultural psychology   The branch of psychology that is primarily concerned with testing possible limitations to knowledge by studying people of different cultures. In its broadest sense, cross-cultural psychology is concerned with the understanding of truth and psychological principles as either universal (true for all people of all cultures) or culture-specific (true for some people of some cultures).

cross-cultural research   Research that involves participants from different cultural backgrounds and the testing of possible differences among these `groups of participants.

culture   The set of attitudes, values, beliefs, and behaviors, shared by a group of people, communicated from one generation to the next via language or some other means of communication (Barnouw, 1985).

emic   Findings that appear to be different across cultures; an emic, therefore, refers to truths that are culture-specific.

ethnocentrism   The inability to separate ourselves from our own cultural backgrounds and biases to understand the behaviors of others.

etic   Findings that appear to be consistent across different cultures; that is, an etic refers to a universal truth or principle.

psychological truth   A statement of fact or knowledge about human behavior that is documented through systematic research and replicated many times.

response sets   The tendency of members of a culture to use certain response alternatives on a questionnaire or in interviews.

stereotypes   Widely held beliefs that people have certain characteristics because of their membership in a particular group.

Suggested Readings

Berry, J. W., Poortinga, Y. H., Segall, M. H., & Dasen, P. R. (1992). *Cross-cultural psychology: Research and applications*. New York: Cambridge University Press.

Brislin, R. (1993). *Understanding culture's influence on behavior*. Fort Worth, TX: Harcourt Brace Jovanovich.

Burlew, A. K. H., Banks, W. C., McAdoo, H. P., & Azibo, D. A. (1992). *African American psychology*. Newbury Park, CA: Sage.

Hofstede, G. (1984). *Culture's consequences*. Newbury Park, CA: Sage.

2

Culture and Self

In Western culture, the notion of self is an abstract statement or proposition about the self, such as "I am sociable." Each of us creates such abstract knowledge about ourselves by considering our own past behaviors and generalizing from them. This abstract knowledge serves to organize and guide our current and future behaviors. For example, you may refer to this knowledge of "me" as "sociable" to decide whether you would attend a party on Saturday night or stay home and read a book.

People from different cultures than our own, however, may disagree with this definition of self and insist that such oversimplified statements about oneself do not do justice to the full complexity of social life. After all, whether someone is sociable or not might depend on the particular situation. From this perspective, such abstract knowledge about the self is inaccurate at best, and believing it could amount ultimately to self-deception or hypocrisy.

This difference illustrates that even though the notion of "self" in its barest form exists almost universally across cultures, what people actually mean and understand by this notion is dramatically different across cultures. In Western, mostly middle-class culture, self is seen as a bounded entity consisting of a number of internal attributes, including needs, abilities, motives, and rights. Each individual carries and uses these internal attributes in navigating thought and action in different social situations. A noted anthropologist, Clifford Geertz (1975), observed nearly two decades ago that the self is seen as

> . . . a bounded, unique, more or less integrated motivational and cognitive universe, a dynamic center of awareness, emotion, judgment, and action organized into a distinctive whole and set contrastively both against other such wholes and against a social and natural background. (p. 48)

15

Suppose a student says that she is "sociable." She is likely to mean much more than what this single word literally denotes. In fact, a whole array of covert meanings or connotations is probably attached to it. Probably, she is implying that (1) she has this attribute within her, just as she possesses other related attributes such as abilities, rights, and interests; (2) her past actions, feelings, or thoughts have close connections with this attribute; and, moreover, (3) her future actions, plans, feelings, or thoughts will be controlled or guided by this attribute and more or less accurately predicted by it. In short, in her mind her concept of herself as "sociable" may be rooted in, supported by, and reinforced by a rich repertoire of specific information concerning her own actions, thoughts, feelings, motives, and plans. As such, the concept of her self as "sociable" may be very central to her self-definition, enjoying a special status as a salient identity (Stryker, 1986) or self-schema (Markus, 1977).

People of other cultures, however, may not fathom this idea implicit in the Western concept of the self. They may not grasp intuitively the idea of an elaborate array of self-relevant knowledge underlying the simple summary statement "I am sociable." In fact, it may require a considerable stretch of these people's imaginations to even entertain the possibility that a self-concept could entail such connotations and could guide or organize their behaviors.

By raising the possibility that the Western concept of self may not make much intuitive sense to people of other cultures, I do not wish to imply that students of other cultures, let alone experts in social psychology, fail to understand the foregoing notion of self as a theoretical concept in social psychology. To the contrary, they certainly can and do understand the notion as a theoretical construct. Yet the nature of their understanding is very different from that of the American undergraduate. Non-Westerners may understand Western concepts of self only as much as we Americans may understand four-dimensional space, and vice versa. That is, we may understand concepts of self from other cultures on a theoretical level, but we have almost no experiential basis for understanding them.

This chapter will look at different construals, or understandings, of the self. It will contrast the Western construal of self as an independent, separate entity with another construal of self that is more common in many non-Western cultures. According to this latter construal, the person is viewed as inherently connected or interdependent with others and inseparable from a social context. The chapter will illustrate how these divergent forms of self are tied to differences in what people notice and think about, how they feel, and what motivates them. Because notions of self are so central to psychological health and adjustment, it is extremely important to gain a better understanding of how self-concepts themselves may be bounded or influenced by culture. It is also especially important to consider how these cultural differences in notions of self have an impact on the way we think, the emotions we feel, and how we are motivated to do things in our lives.

Two Construals of Self

There are many anecdotes to suggest that construals of self vary widely across cultures. In America, standing out and asserting oneself is a virtue. It is "the squeaky wheel that gets the grease." In many Asian cultures, however, if you stand out, you will most likely be punished—"the nail that sticks up shall get pounded down."

In this section, we describe two different construals of self. To be sure, the world is not a dichotomy, and everyone cannot be pigeonholed into one of these two categories. Instead, we use these categories to exemplify two possible extremes—of many different possibilities—of cultural differences in notions of self. You can use these as a platform to entertain and discuss culturally different notions of self.

Independent Construal of Self

In many Western cultures there is a strong belief in separateness among distinct individuals. The normative task of these cultures is to maintain the independence of the individual as a separate, self-contained entity. In American society, for example, many of us have been socialized to "be unique," "express yourself," "realize and actualize the inner self," "promote your own goals," and so on. The culture provides these tasks for its members, and they have been designed and selected, through history, to encourage the independence of each separate self. With this set of cultural tasks, our sense of self-worth or self-esteem takes on a particular form. When individuals successfully carry out these cultural tasks, they feel most satisfied about themselves. Their self-esteem increases accordingly. Under this independent construal of self, individuals tend to focus on internal attributes such as one's own ability, intelligence, personality traits, goals, preferences, or attributes, expressing them in public and verifying and confirming them in private through social comparison.

The independent construal of self is graphically illustrated in Figure 2.1(a). Self is a bounded entity, clearly separated from relevant others. Note that there is no overlap between self and the others. Furthermore, the most salient self-relevant information (indicated by bold Xs) consists of the attributes that are thought to be stable, constant, and intrinsic to the self, such as abilities, goals, rights, and the like. As such, these attributes are bound to be quite general and abstract.

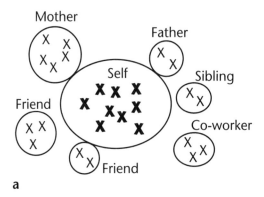

a

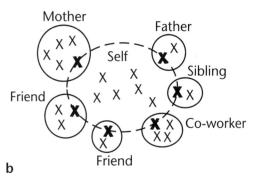

b

Figure 2.1 **(a)** Independent Construal of Self; **(b)** Interdependent Construal of Self. (From Markus, H., & Kitayama, S. (1991). Culture and the self: Implications for cognition, emotion and motivation. *Psychological Review, 98,* 224–253. Copyright 1991 by the American Psychological Association. Reprinted by permission of the authors.)

Interdependent Construal of Self

By contrast, many non-Western cultures neither assume nor value this overt separateness. Instead, these cultures emphasize what may be called the "fundamental connectedness of human beings." The primary normative task is to adjust oneself so as to fit in and maintain the interdependence among individuals. Thus, many individuals in these cultures are socialized to "adjust oneself to an attendant relationship or a group to which they belong," "read others' minds," "be sympathetic," "occupy and play one's assigned role," "engage in appropriate actions," and the like. These are the cultural tasks that have been designed and selected through the history of a given cultural group to encourage the interdependence of the self with others.

Given this construal of the self, one's sense of worth, satisfaction, or self-esteem can have very different characteristics from those familiar to us in the Western culture. The self-esteem of those with interdependent construals of the self may depend primarily on whether one can fit in and be part of a relevant ongoing relationship. Under this construal of self, individuals tend to focus on their interdependent status with other people and strive to meet or even create duties, obligations, and social responsibilities. Accordingly, the most salient aspect of the conscious experience is intersubjective—rooted in finely tuned interpersonal relationships.

The interdependent construal of self is graphically illustrated in Figure 2.1(b). Self is unbounded, flexible, and contingent on context, as indicated by the substantial overlaps between self and relevant others. The most salient information about self (bold *X*s) concerns aspects of the self-in-relationships—that is, those features of the self related to and inseparable from specific social contexts.

This does not mean, of course, that those with interdependent selves do not have any knowledge about their internal attributes such as personality traits, abilities, attitudes, and the like. They clearly do. These internal attributes, however, are relatively less salient in consciousness and thus unlikely to be the primary concerns in thinking, feeling, and acting.

Of course, any single culture can also have considerable variations among its members in their independent versus interdependent construals of the self. People of different ethnicities within a culture, for example, may have different tendencies with regard to independent versus interdependent self-construals. Men and women have different self-construals. Even within ethnic and gender groups, there can and will be considerable differences in self-construals (Gilligan, 1982; Joseph, Markus, & Tafarodi, 1992). No doubt these differences are also important in our considerations of cultural differences. This chapter describes *general* tendencies associated with independent and interdependent self-construals, acknowledging the limitations in representation within groups.

Consequences for Cognition, Motivation, and Emotion

Learning about these potentially different notions of self can be very useful in our lives today. This section examines how the two construals of the self affect our thinking, feelings, and behaviors. As you will see, cognitive, emotional, and motivational processes can vary dramatically according to the construal of the self shared within a cultural group.

Consequences for Cognition

Self-perception.   Different construals of self have different consequences for how we perceive ourselves. With an independent construal of self, one's internal attributes such as abilities or personality traits are the most salient, self-relevant information. These internal attributes should be relatively less salient for those with interdependent selves, who are more likely to think about the self in particular social relationships (for example, "me" with family members, "me" with my boyfriend) or in specific contexts ("me" in school, "me" at work).

This analysis has received support from several studies. In these studies subjects are asked to write down as many of their characteristics as possible. Subjects typically write several types of responses. One type is abstract personality-trait descriptions of the self, such as "I am sociable." Another type of response is self-descriptions that are situation-specific. Consistent with our views of independent and interdependent selves, studies have shown that American subjects tend to write a greater number of abstract traits than do Asian subjects (Bond & Tak-Sing, 1983; Shweder & Bourne, 1984).

This, of course, does not mean that Americans have more knowledge about themselves than do Asians. Because the most salient information about self for the interdependent selves is context-specific, these individuals must have found it difficult or unnatural to state anything in abstract, noncontextual terms. Instead, those with interdependent selves may be bound to define themselves in very different terms.

Consistent with this analysis, Triandis (1989) and colleagues have shown that individuals from interdependent cultures (such as China, Japan, and Korea) generate many more social categories, relationships, or groups to which they belong. Indeed, in a study done in the People's Republic of China, as many as 80% of all the responses to the self-description task were about their memberships in a variety of groups. This is a strong indication that specific relationships are very important in their self-definitions.

There is yet another interesting implication. If people with interdependent senses of self find it difficult to describe themselves in terms of abstract internal attributes, they should be comfortable in describing themselves in terms of abstract, internal attributes once a specific context has been specified. In a recent experiment, Cousins (1989) provided evidence to support this analysis. He asked American and Japanese respondents to write down who they were in various specific social situations (at home, in school, at work, and so on). This instruction supposedly helped the respondents to picture a concrete social situation, including who was there, what was being done to whom, and the like. The Japanese respondents generated a greater number of abstract internal attributes than did the Americans once the context was specified. The American respondents tended to qualify their descriptions—for instance, "I am more or less sociable at work," "I am sometimes optimistic at home." They seemed to be saying, "This is how I am at work, but don't assume that this is the way I am everywhere." For such a contextualized task, the Americans may have felt awkward in providing self-descriptions because their self-definitions typically are not qualified by specific situations.

Social explanation. Self-construals may also serve as a "cognitive template" for perceiving and interpreting behaviors of other people. Those with independent selves may assume that other people will also have a set of relatively stable internal attributes such as personality traits, attitudes, and abilities. As a result, when they observe the behavior of someone else, they may draw inferences about the actor's internal state, or his or her disposition, that supposedly underlies and even caused that behavior.

Social cognition research done primarily in the West has supported this claim. For example, when subjects read an essay supporting Fidel Castro in Cuba (Jones & Harris, 1967), they inferred that the author must have a favorable attitude toward Castro. Furthermore, it has been amply demonstrated that such dispositional inferences occur even when obvious situational constraints are present. In the original study by Jones and Harris (1967), the subjects inferred the pro-Castro attitude even when they were explicitly told that the author was assigned to write a pro-Castro essay and no choice was given. The subjects ignored these situational constraints and erroneously drew inferences about the author's intentions. This bias to commit an inference about an actor's dispositions even in the presence of very obvious situational constraints has been termed the **fundamental attribution error** (Ross, 1977).

Fundamental attribution error, however, may not be as robust or pervasive among people of interdependent cultures. People in these cultures share assumptions about the self that are very different from those in Western cultures. This construal includes the recognition that what one does is contingent or dependent on, and directed or guided by, situational factors. Thus, these individuals are more inclined to explain another's behaviors in terms of situational forces impinging on the person, rather than on internal predispositions.

In an important cross-cultural study, Miller (1984) examined patterns of social explanation in Americans and Hindu Indians. First, both Indian and American respondents were asked to describe either someone they knew well who did something good for another person, or someone they knew well who did something bad to another person. After having described such a person, the respondents were asked to explain why the person committed that good or bad action. The American respondents typically explained the behavior of their acquaintances in terms of general dispositions (for example, "she is very irresponsible"). Dispositional explanations, however, were much less common for the Indians. Instead, they tended to provide explanations in terms of the actor's duties, social roles, and the like, which are by definition more situation-specific (see also Shweder & Bourne, 1984).

Some writers (Lively & Bromley, 1973) have suggested another explanation for these results, based on Piaget's theory of intellectual development. In a nutshell, Piaget (1952, 1954) suggested that humans go through various stages of intellectual development, which generally proceed from "concrete operations" to higher stages of "abstract operations." Using this theory as a framework, some theorists have suggested that non-Western people (such as the Hindu Indian adults in the study described) are less developed intellectually than American adults. As a result, the Indians used situation-specific, concrete terms, whereas Americans used more abstract trait terms in social explanations.

This explanation, however, may be ethnocentric. Whenever we characterize other cultures in a way that places them in an inferior position to our own, we have to be careful. Indeed, the theory may reflect our desire to see ourselves in a favorable light. In this case, our realization of different self-construals accounts for why Indians may not seek to explain social behaviors in abstract terms, even if they are fully capable of abstract reasoning. They find it unreasonable or unnatural to explain others' and their own behaviors in abstract dispositional terms. Still, are there data that rule out differences as a function of cognitive ability?

Fortunately, Miller (1984) collected data from people of different social classes and educational attainment and showed that the Indian tendency toward situation-specific explanations did not depend on these factors. Thus, it is very unlikely that the situational, context-specific thinking common among Indians was due to an inability to reason abstractly. Instead, the context-specific reasoning common in India seems to be due primarily to the cultural assumption of interdependence that is very salient in the Hindu culture. Given the interdependent construal of self, the most reasonable assumption to be made in explaining another's behavior is that this behavior is very much constrained and directed by situation-specific factors.

Consequences for Emotion

Social connotation of emotion.   Kitayama and Markus (in press, a) have distinguished emotions that encourage the independence of the self from those that encourage interdependence. For example, some emotions such as pride or feelings of superiority occur when one has accomplished one's own goals or desires, or has confirmed desirable inner attributes such as intelligence and wealth. The experience of these emotions tends to verify those inner attributes. Similarly, some negative emotions such as anger and frustration result primarily from the blocking of one's own internal attributes (such as goals or desires). Once experienced, the negative emotions highlight the fact that those inner goals or desires have been interfered with.

In both cases, one's inner attributes are made salient and contrasted against relevant social context. These emotions therefore tend to separate or disengage the self from social relationships. They also simultaneously promote the perceived independence of the self from the relationship. Kitayama and Markus (in press,a) have called these types of emotions **socially disengaged emotions.**

By contrast, other positive emotions, such as friendly feelings and feelings of respect, are very different in this regard. They result from being part of a close, more or less communal relationship. Once experienced, they further encourage this interpersonal bond. Some types of negative emotions, such as feelings of indebtedness or guilt, also share similar characteristics. These emotions typically result from one's failure to participate successfully in an interdependent relationship, or from doing some harm to the relationship. Once these emotions are experienced, one is subsequently motivated to restore the harmony in the relationship by compensating for the harm done or by repaying one's debt. These behaviors will further engage and assimilate the self in the relationship and thus enhance the perceived interdependence of the self with the relevant others. These emotions are called **socially engaged emotions.**

All people, regardless of their self-construals, will experience both types of emotions. What is different, however, is the definitions that are associated with social engagement or disengagement, and the social meanings and consequences of the emotions. People of interdependent self-construals will typically experience socially engaged emotions differently than will people of independent self-construals. These emotions may be more intense and internalized for the interdependent selves than for the independent selves, because socially engaged emotions have different implications for interdependent selves as opposed to independent selves. The same is true for socially disengaged emotions.

Self-construals and happiness. There are additional cross-cultural differences in emotional experience. One of these concerns the meaning of happiness. "Happiness" refers to the most generic, unqualified state of "feeling good." Emotions such as relaxed, elated, and calm are part of this generic, positive state. People across cultures share the general notion of happiness as defined in this way (Wierzbicka, 1986). But the specific circumstances, and the meanings attached to them, may depend crucially on the construal of the self as independent or interdependent. Specifically, evidence suggests that people experience this most unqualified, good feeling when they have successfully accomplished the cultural task of either independence or interdependence.

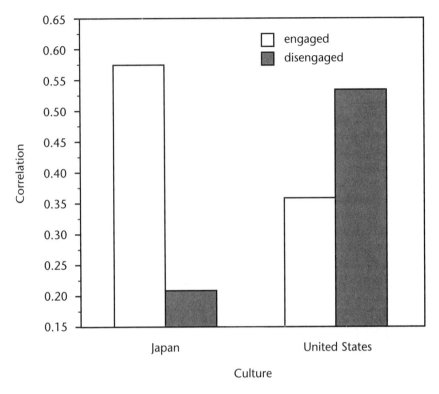

Figure 2.2 Cultural Differences in the Correlation Between General Positive Feelings and Engaged and Disengaged Emotions in the United States and Japan

Kitayama, Markus, Kurokawa, and Negishi (1993) asked both Japanese and American college undergraduates to report how frequently they experience various emotions. Among them were three types of positive emotions. Some were generic, such as relaxed, elated, and calm. Others had more specific social connotations either as socially engaged (for example, friendly feelings, feelings of respect) or disengaged (pride, feelings of superiority). An interesting cross-cultural difference emerged when correlations among these three types of emotions were examined (see Figure 2.2).

For Americans, generic positive emotions were associated primarily with experiencing the disengaged emotions. That is, those who experience the emotions that signal their success in cultural tasks of independence (socially disengaged emotions such as pride) are most likely to feel "generally good." This pattern was completely reversed among the Japanese. Those who experience the emotions that signal success in cultural tasks of interdependence (socially engaged emotions such as friendly feelings) are most likely to feel "generally good." The exact meanings or connotations of "feeling good" were shaped through culture and linked very closely with the cultural imperatives of independence (in the United States) and interdependence (in Japan).

Consequences for Motivation

Western literature on motivation has long assumed that motivations are basically internal to the actor. One's motives to achieve, affiliate, or dominate are some of the most salient and important features of the internal self—features that direct and energize overt behaviors. With an alternative, interdependent construal, however, social behaviors are guided by expectations of relevant others, felt obligations to the others, or the sense of duties to an important group to which one belongs, rather than by motivations for "me." This point is illustrated by two topics that have received considerable research attention: achievement motivation and self-enhancement versus effacement.

Achievement motivation.   **Achievement motivation** refers to a "desire for excellence." Such a desire in the broad sense can be found quite widely across cultures (Maehr & Nicholls, 1980). In the current literature, however, this desire for excellence has been conceptualized in a somewhat more specific manner—as individually or personally based, rather than socially or interpersonally rooted. In classic work in this area by McClelland (1961) and Atkinson (1964), for example, the desire for excellence is linked very closely with one's tendency to push oneself ahead and actively strive for and seek individual successes. This notion of achievement, in fact, is quite congruent with an independent construal of the self, shared widely in the West.

From an alternative, interdependent frame, however, excellence may be sought through broader social goals. These social forms of achievement motivation are more prevalent among those with an interdependent construal of the self. Interdependent selves have ever-important concerns that revolve around fully realizing one's connectedness with others. Thus, the nature of their achievement motivation is quite different from that of those with an independent construal of the self.

Discussing this possibility with respect to the Chinese, Yang (1982) distinguished between two forms of achievement motivation: individually oriented and socially oriented (cf. Maehr & Nicholls, 1980). Individually oriented achievement is considered to be common primarily in Western culture. It is for the sake of "me" personally that one strives to achieve. In Chinese society, however, socially oriented achievement is much more common. According to this form of achievement, one strives to achieve for the sake of relevant others, such as one's family members. A

Chinese student, for example, may work hard to gain admission to a prestigious university and then eventually to a top company. Behaviorally, there may be no difference between this Chinese individual and an American with an independent sense of self. In the case of the Chinese individual, however, the ultimate goal in doing all this may not be advancement of one's personal career, but rather enhancing his or her family's social standing, meeting a felt expectation of the family members, or satisfying a sense of obligation or indebtedness to parents who have made enormous sacrifices to raise and support the student. In other words, the Chinese student's desire to achieve is much more socially rooted and may not necessarily reflect his or her desire to advance the quality or standing of himself or herself personally.

In support of this notion, Bond (1986) assessed levels of various motivations among Chinese and found that the Chinese in fact show higher levels of socially oriented rather than individually oriented achievement motivation. Yu (1974) reported that the strength of achievement motive in China is positively related to familism and filial piety. That is, those who are most strongly motivated to excel also take most seriously their duties and obligations to family members, especially parents. K. Doi (1982, 1985) reported that, for Japanese college students, there was a close association between achievement motivation and affiliation—those high in achievement were also high in affiliation, and vice versa. This finding is in stark contrast to many Western findings, which indicate that these two dimensions of motives are typically unrelated (cf. Atkinson, 1964). Both studies of the Chinese and the Japanese indicated that achievement was closely related to their social orientation of being connected and interdependent with important others in life.

Self-enhancement versus effacement. Since James (1890), psychologists have repeatedly demonstrated what appears to be an extremely powerful motive to have a positive view of self. As early as age 4, American children think they are better than most others. Wylie (1979) found that American adults typically consider themselves to be more intelligent and more attractive than average. Myers (1987), in a national survey of American students, found that 70% of the students thought they were above average in leadership ability; with respect to the ability to get along with others, 0% thought they were below average and 60% thought they were in the top 10%. This tendency to underestimate the commonality of one's desirable traits is called the **false uniqueness effect** and appears to be stronger for males than for females (Joseph, Markus, & Tafarodi, 1992). It is one clear method of enhancing self-esteem. But is it true for people of different cultures?

Maintaining or enhancing self may assume a different form for those with interdependent construals of self. Among those with interdependent selves, positive appraisals of the inner attributes of self may not be strongly linked with overall self-esteem or self-satisfaction. Instead, overall self-esteem or self-satisfaction may be more likely to derive from fulfilling one's interdependence with others or from the recognition that one is performing well in the cultural tasks of belonging, fitting in, engaging in appropriate action, promoting others' goals, maintaining harmony, and so on. It may also derive from one's capacity to regulate and coordinate one's inner personal thoughts and feelings so that they can fit into one's pursuit of interdependence with others. For the interdependent selves, viewing oneself as unique or different would be unnecessary to maintain a sense of self-worth. This is because the inner attributes of self contributing to one's perceived uniqueness are less self-defining. Trying to be unique would be undesirable, akin to being the nail that stands out, because it isolates the person from the ever-important relationship.

Markus and Kitayama (1991b) administered questionnaires containing a series of false-uniqueness items to both Japanese and American college students. The questionnaires included a series of questions of the form "What proportion of students in this university have higher intellectual abilities than yourself?" There were three categories of questionnaire items: abilities (intellectual, memory, and athletic), independence (independent, holds more strongly to his or her own view), and interdependence (more sympathetic, more warm-hearted).

The data are summarized in Figure 2.3. The most striking aspect of these data is the marked difference between the Japanese and the American students in their estimations of their own uniqueness. American students assume that only 30% of people on average would be better than themselves in various traits and abilities. The Japanese, however, showed almost no evidence of this false uniqueness. In most cases, they claim that about 50% of students would be better than they are. One might suspect that this occurred because the Japanese students tended to use 50% as their most preferred answer. This was not the case. If anything, the variability in the data was virtually identical for the Americans and the Japanese. Instead, this finding is just what one would predict if a representative sample of college students were evaluating themselves without the need to establish uniqueness.

Conclusion

Self-concepts are crucial in guiding and explaining a variety of individual behaviors. Across cultures, the form of self varies considerably, and various social phenomena and processes also vary accordingly. It is very important for psychologists to examine carefully whether and to what extent various

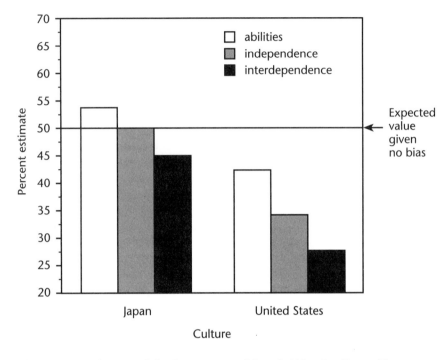

Figure 2.3 Estimates of the Percentage of People Who Are Better Than Oneself in Three Categories of Behavior

social psychological principles—most of which have been advanced in the Western world—can travel across cultural boundaries to account for behaviors of people of other cultures. In so doing, psychologists can identify the phenomena that explain these cultural differences. Self-construal is one such powerful phenomenon, providing a framework by which we can understand and analyze cultural variation in cognition, emotion, and motivation.

Understanding cultural differences in self-construals is particularly important to issues of adjustment. Cultural influences on notions of self provide an important basis by which we can better understand principles of psychology that are useful in our lives. They also provide an important platform with which we can explain when those principles may not be applicable to ourselves or those around us. Recognition of cultural differences in the sense of self also helps us to loosen the grip of ethnocentrism and cultural filters on our interpretations of the behaviors of others around us. This recognition can lead to better relationships with others and a better understanding of ourselves.

Still, this task is not easy. Our cultural filters are *always* there and *always* influence how we perceive and evaluate things, regardless of whether we are aware of it or not. You are reading this text right now with that filter on. We make judgments about ourselves and others that are totally biased, even if we are absolutely convinced that we are unbiased in making those judgments. For example, you may believe that you are rather interdependent, not independent, and that your behaviors take social relations into account much more than do the behaviors of your peers. Still, the culture in which you live may be as a whole more independent than other cultures. Although you are relatively interdependent within your own culture, you may still be *very* independent when viewed in comparison to the rest of the world. And yet, you may absolutely believe that you are interdependent, because you cannot see the implicit standard of your own culture in relation to the standard provided by the rest of the world (cf. Kitayama & Markus, in press, b). Many years ago, Durkheim (1938/1964) wrote, "Air is no less heavy because we do not detect its weight" (p. 5). Likewise, water is no less important to fish because they may not be aware of its existence. Culture is that air for us, and water for the fish.

Glossary

achievement motivation   Motivation that underlies a "desire for excellence."

false uniqueness effect   The tendency to underestimate the commonality of one's desirable traits.

fundamental attribution error   A bias to commit an inference about an actor's dispositions even in the presence of very obvious situational constraints.

independent construal of self   A framework that views the self as a bounded entity, clearly separated from relevant others. The most salient, self-relevant information are the attributes that are thought to be stable, constant, and intrinsic to the self, such as abilities, goals, rights, and the like. These attributes are bound to be quite general and abstract.

indigenous emotions   Emotions that are relatively unique to particular cultures.

interdependent construal of self   A framework that views the self as influenced by the "fundamental connectedness of human beings." The primary normative task is to adjust oneself so as to fit in and maintain the interdependence among individuals. Self is unbounded, flexible, and contingent on context. The most salient information about self is about aspects of the self-in-relationships—that is, those features of the self related to and inseparable from specific social contexts.

self-perception   How we perceive ourselves.

social explanation   The process of perceiving and interpreting behaviors of other people; also known as *attributions*.

socially disengaged emotions   Emotions that tend to separate or disengage the self from social relationships. They simultaneously promote the perceived independence of the self from the relationship.

socially engaged emotions   Emotions that have high interpersonal meanings, either encouraging or harming interpersonal bonds. By serving as motivators of behaviors that will further engage and assimilate the self into a social relationship, they enhance the perceived interdependence of the self with the relevant others.

Suggested Readings

Berman, J. J. (Ed.). (1989). *Cross-cultural perspectives, Nebraska Symposium on Motivation, 1989.* Lincoln: University of Nebraska Press.

Kitayama, S., & Markus, H. R. (in press). A cultural perspective to self-conscious emotions. In J. P. Tangney & K. Fisher (Eds.), *Shame, guilt, embarrassment, and pride: Empirical studies of self-conscious emotions.* New York: Guilford Press.

Markus, H. R., & Kitayama, S. (1991). Culture and the self: Implications for cognition, emotion, and motivation. *Psychological Review, 98,* 224–253.

Shweder, R. A., & Bourne, E. J. (1984). Does the concept of the person vary cross-culturally? In R. A. Shweder & R. A. LeVine (Eds.), *Culture theory: Essays on mind, self, and emotion* (pp. 158–199). Cambridge, England: Cambridge University Press.

Triandis, H. C. (1989). The self and social behavior in differing cultural contexts. *Psychological Review, 96,* 506–520.

3

Culture and Communication

Communication is an integral aspect of our daily lives. Good communication is crucial to maintaining good relationships with others, whether at work, play, or home. Marital satisfaction is highly dependent on good communication processes, as are work relationships. Good communication skills can also be a source of self-satisfaction.

Communication is especially important to culture because it is a necessary component of culture itself. That is, culture is transmitted, in large part, from one generation to the next via some communication process. This process may be in the form of verbal language, with caretakers and peers teaching the rules of culture through an oral tradition. This communication process can also be nonverbal, however, through observation of one's family members and others in society. As discussed in Chapter 1, the very definition of culture is dependent on the transmission of rules, attitudes, beliefs, norms, and behaviors from one generation to the next. Thus, communication processes have an impact on culture.

Culture also has an important influence on communication. Culture influences the structure of verbal language—the grammar, syntax, and sentence structure of the language of that culture. Culture influences the terms of address that you use in interpersonal interaction. Because culture influences our language, culture also influences the way in which we think, because language influences the way we think. Culture influences the rules governing the use of all the various nonverbal channels of communication as well, from the use of gestures, body posture, and interpersonal space to facial expressions, paralanguage, and gaze. In short, culture influences all of our communication processes, both verbal and nonverbal.

Understanding the influence of culture on language and communication is extremely important in our multicultural world today. Many of our interactions are with people from cultural backgrounds different than our own. They come not only speaking different verbal languages, but also operating under different rules of nonverbal behaviors and thinking in fundamentally different ways because of the structure of their language. Even if you meet people who speak fluent English verbally, they may engage in nonverbal behaviors that you might think are inappropriate or difficult to interpret. Or they may not interpret the same words in the same way you do. Recognizing these potential differences and difficulties is a key first step to engaging in better communication with people from all cultures and achieving better psychological adjustment.

This chapter focuses on nonverbal behaviors. This is not to minimize the importance of verbal language, but rather to give you an idea of the subtlety, and complexity, of the influence of culture on the entire communication process, using some nonverbal channels as an example. Let's begin, however, by exploring in more detail what nonverbal behaviors are.

What Are Nonverbal Behaviors?

When people think about communication, they generally think about language. But language is just one part of communication. In fact, it may be the smallest component of communication. We use many other vehicles of expression to communicate our thoughts, feelings, desires, and wishes to others. These other vehicles are not language; that is, they are not words or sentences. In short, they are not verbal. They are nonverbal. In the broadest sense, **nonverbal behaviors** are all the behaviors other than words that occur during communication. Facial expressions are examples of nonverbal behaviors. The movements of our hands, arms, and legs are nonverbal behaviors. Our postures are nonverbal behaviors. Even characteristics of our voices above and beyond the words we speak are nonverbal behaviors. Indeed, the term *nonverbal behaviors* captures a whole range of behaviors associated with communication, including behaviors we typically associate with active expressivity, such as facial expressions, gestures, posture, and voice characteristics. But there is a whole world of more subtle behaviors associated with nonverbal behavior and communication as well. These include the use of space and interpersonal distance, gaze behavior and visual attention, the use of time, the type of clothing we wear, and the type of architectural structures we have and use around us.

All these different types of behavior fall under the general category of nonverbal behaviors. When you stop to think of all the different things that are actually occurring when people communicate with each other, it is mind-boggling. People come to an interaction in a certain place that is bounded by how they have structured it physically. They come to that interaction with a certain appearance. They space themselves from one another at certain distances. They adopt certain postures when interacting. They gesture and use hand movements to illustrate what they are saying. Their faces may become animated or reserved. Their voices may become excited or suppressed. Indeed, when communication is occurring, the actual words and language used are only a small part of the entire package of events and behaviors that constitute communication. It is no wonder that several studies have reported that only a small fraction of the meaning people get in an interaction is based on the words that were spoken. In fact, most of the messages conveyed and perceived in interactions are nonverbal (see, for example, Mehrabian, 1981).

Culture, Nonverbal Behaviors, and Communication

Just as spoken languages differ from one culture to the next, so do unspoken, nonverbal behaviors. People of all cultures learn to use nonverbal behaviors—facial expressions, gestures, distance, gaze, and postures—as part of their communication repertoire, but people in each culture learn to use them in very specific ways. All humans are born with the capacity to form all types of sounds; culture dictates how we shape and mold those sounds into particular languages. In this same way, culture shapes and molds nonverbal behaviors into each culture's nonverbal language.

Consider, for example, our American culture. We all have a certain way of dressing for school or for business. When we speak to someone, we look them straight in the eye. Our faces and gestures often become animated, highlighting specific, important parts of our speech. We learn to sit or stand at a certain distance when we interact, depending on with whom we are interacting and the specific context or situation in which that interaction is occurring. We learn how to signal when we are finished speaking and when we want to continue speaking. In short, we learn a very specific, American system of nonverbal behaviors to aid in our communication process, just as we have learned American English as a verbal language.

When we interact with people from our own culture, they have generally learned the same system or language of nonverbal behaviors. They will most likely follow the same rules of dress, manner, appearance, distance, tone of voice, facial expressions, gestures, and postures. When we interact with longtime friends, for example, we know what that system is (even though we may not be able to verbalize it), and we can interact with them successfully, being unambiguous with regard to the content of the message or its intent.

The same is true for our families. Our family members generally "speak" the same nonverbal language we do. After all, it is from these families that we learned our nonverbal language. When we interact with them, there are relatively fewer instances when we are unable to read or correctly interpret the meaning of the nonverbal signals we receive from all the various nonverbal channels.

The power of culture can be seen when we interact with people from our own culture who may be totally unfamiliar to us. When we meet someone for the first time, at a party, a business engagement, on the street, or in the theater, we can usually engage in some kind of conversation where we can successfully interpret the nonverbal messages being conveyed. Their nonverbal behaviors may be coy, flirtatious, or annoying—just about anything.

The point is that we have all learned the same rules of making and interpreting nonverbal behaviors. When we see a certain action or behavior, we have learned how to interpret it, according to an implicit and informal set of guidelines dictated by our culture-specific nonverbal language. When the rules by which someone is engaging in nonverbal behaviors and language are the same as the rules by which another person is interpreting those behaviors, everything is fine. Interaction comes off smoothly and successfully, with little ambiguity about intent or message.

Now consider a situation where you are interacting with someone from a different culture. People from another culture bring with them their own verbal language. A person from Israel, for example, will bring the ability to speak Hebrew. A person from India will bring the ability to speak Hindi or a provincial dialect of India. But beyond the culture-specific verbal language they bring with them, they also bring a culture-specific nonverbal language. Thus, people from Israel will bring with them the Israeli- or Jewish-specific language of nonverbal behaviors; people from India will bring with them the India-specific language of nonverbal behaviors. When you stop to think about it, there are really two languages occurring in all types of interactions—one verbal and one nonverbal.

People from different cultures have their own rules for engaging in nonverbal behaviors. These rules may be quite different from the rules you or I may be fluent in. These rules may dictate that different behaviors are enacted to get a certain point across or to accent a specific point. These rules may mean that the same behavior can actually carry quite different meanings.

Just as people from different cultures have their own rules for engaging in nonverbal behaviors, they have their own rules for interpreting the nonverbal behaviors of others. Obviously, they will have learned to associate certain behaviors with certain meanings, and these associations or relationships are all dependent on their culture and its rules.

When we interact with people from a different culture, most of the time we try to attend most closely to the verbal language. But nonverbal language is also occurring. Just because we don't attend to it consciously as much does not mean that it is not occurring. Nonverbal language continues, like verbal language. The unconscious filters and processes we have learned so we can automatically interpret the nonverbal behaviors of people from our own culture are also occurring; they do not stop.

The problem in intercultural communication is that these nonverbal languages are silent. Our interpretational processes are unconscious and automatic. We may not attend to them very much, but messages are being transmitted. More often than not, the nonverbal language of people of a different culture is different from what we are accustomed to. After interacting with people from another culture, it is not uncommon to wonder whether you really "got" what was meant. Oftentimes we leave these situations feeling that we may have missed something. These feelings arise because our unconscious system of nonverbal communication is having difficulty interpreting the nonverbal behaviors of the people from a different culture. Something just doesn't "feel" right. The "aftertaste" of these interactions leaves you thinking.

Problems occur in the opposite direction as well. People often interpret certain types of behaviors positively when, in fact, they are not meant to be positive at all. Consider, for example, the Japanese head nodding and the use of the word *hai*. The best translation of this word in English is "yes." But in Japanese this word does not necessarily mean yes. It may mean yes, but it can also mean maybe, or even no. It is often used as a speech **regulator**, informing the speaker that the listener is listening. It can be a signal of deference to authority. This word and the nonverbal behaviors associated with it (head nod) definitely do not have the same meaning in Japanese as they do in English. Yet many business and government negotiations have faltered on the interpretation of exactly this behavior, with Americans believing that the Japanese have agreed to something and that the deal is closed. The Japanese, however, may merely be signaling that they are listening. This type of cultural difference is the source of many interpersonal conflicts between spouses and lovers as well.

When we interact with people who have different nonverbal languages, we often form negative impressions of them. In the United States, we all learn to interact with people at a certain distance. When you interact with someone you do not know very well and this person places himself close enough to you so you feel his breath when he speaks, you will probably feel quite uncomfortable and try to adjust the distance. He will follow. You will adjust again. He will follow again. You will probably want to get out of that interaction as soon as possible. When you do, you will think that the person was rude or without manners. Many Arab and Middle Eastern cultures foster what we Americans would consider too close interpersonal spacing during interactions and this can be unsettling.

Or consider the opposite scenario. You are interacting with someone who stands quite far away from you, farther than you think would be normal under the circumstances. When you try to get closer, she moves farther away. You move up again; she moves back again. Afterwards, you will probably think she had a negative impression of you and didn't really want to interact with you.

We make these interpretations because we are trying to match observed behavior with our own rules for what those behaviors should mean. If the people described earlier were indeed from your own culture and operated according to the same rules, you would probably be correct in your interpretations. But what if those people were from a different culture and operated under different rules? Then your negative impressions and interpretations of their behaviors might be totally off base. Yet you have those impressions and interpretations, and you leave feeling bad about the interaction, probably not wanting to interact any more. The others probably feel the same way.

Nonverbal behaviors are just like a second language, albeit a silent, unspoken language. Just as cultures develop spoken, verbal languages, they also develop unspoken, nonverbal languages. These nonverbal languages are just as important, if not more so, to the overall communication process. If we are to get a handle on cultural similarities and differences in communication, we obviously need to pay more attention to cultural differences in these silent, nonverbal languages.

Cultural Differences in Nonverbal Behaviors

If you were to take a trip to another country or had visitors from another country coming to stay with you or you just wanted to learn another language, what might you do? One of the things you might consider is going to your local bookstore, finding the reference or language section, and searching through the various types of language learning books or dictionaries for sale for your particular language of interest. You'd search through some of the alternatives that were for sale, find one you like, and buy it. With dictionary in hand, you would be able to look up words or phrases you want to say. When someone speaks to you in that language, you can look up what they were saying to you or have them find the passage and point it out to you.

Wouldn't it be great if dictionaries existed for the silent, nonverbal languages of the world as well? There could be a book or videotape reference containing all the possible nonverbal behaviors in a certain language and their translation in English and the American nonverbal system. If you saw some behaviors or noticed a certain expression when interacting with someone from another culture, you could look it up and find out what it might mean instead of trying to interpret those behaviors according to your own, implicit, nonverbal language dictionary.

Fortunately, there has been a considerable amount of research on nonverbal behaviors and how cultures differ in the use of them. This research has spanned a number of topics and types of nonverbal behaviors, including gaze and visual behavior, interpersonal space and proxemics, gestures, postures, nonverbal vocal cues, facial expressions, the use of time, clothing, touch, and even smell. Studies in each of these various areas have produced a wealth of information about the complexity and importance of nonverbal behaviors in interpersonal communication and interaction.

The remainder of this chapter will focus on three specific nonverbal behaviors—gaze and visual attention, interpersonal space, and gestures. I selected these topics for several reasons. First of all, there is a substantial base of cross-cultural research in each of these areas to inform us of how culture influences these aspects of the communication process. Also, these are primary areas of concern and interest in interpersonal interaction episodes and have the greatest relevance to our understanding and appreciation of cultural differences in communication styles. One other major channel of nonverbal behavior, facial expressions, is generally described well in most standard texts, along with the mechanism for culturally based differences in facial expressions: display rules.

Gaze and Visual Behavior

In learning about cultures and how they influence human behavior, from time to time it is useful to look at research findings not with humans but with animals that have relevance to our understanding of possible universal and culture-specific aspects of behavior. If we reviewed research on nonhuman primates (for example, apes, chimpanzees, gorillas) and found that these animals engaged in many behaviors similar to those of humans, we would certainly begin to wonder if those behaviors might have evolutionary or biological bases. At the very least, these studies would help us gain a broad perspective of the nature of our behaviors and how much they are influenced by culture.

This is especially true of research on gaze and visual attention. A considerable number of studies on gaze and visual behaviors in nonhuman primates force us to think about whether some of our behaviors may be "built into" our behavioral systems. Researchers as early as the 1960s, for example, showed how mutual gazing between animals, especially staring, is a primary and important component of aggressive and threatening displays. The relationship between staring and aggression has been observed in male baboons, gorillas, rhesus and bonnet macaques, and old world monkeys and apes (Altman, 1962; Hall & Devore, 1965; Hinde & Rowell, 1962; Schaller, 1963, 1964; Simonds, 1965; van Hooff, 1967).

This type of research formed much of the basis of our knowledge about what is known as attention structures in animal societies. An **attention structure** is an organized pattern that dictates which animals can look at others, and vice versa. Attention structures appear to be highly related to dominance hierarchies in animal societies. In general, comparative research on nonhuman primates has shown that animals with lower status and power in a group pay more attention to higher status animals and adjust their behaviors accordingly.

Let's switch our attention temporarily back to humans. Have you ever played a game of staring? This game has several different names, depending on the time period and geographic area of the United States in question, but it involves two interactants staring at each other with a blank or neutral face. The game proceeds until one of the two people looks away, starts laughing, or generally breaks off the stare. The one who breaks off the stare is the loser.

This game exemplifies some of the dominance, status, and power themes associated with gaze and found in the animal literature. In animal research, it has been shown that animals, too, have a dominance or power struggle that involves mutual glaring or staring at each other (Fehr & Exline, 1987). The power struggle between two animals will end when one of the animals backs off and breaks the gaze. We seem to have a taboo against these types of direct stares, as if our cultures produce rules by which we can curb or control such displays of aggression or dominance.

Dominance and aggression, however, are not the only messages that gazing gives. Some writers (for example, Argyle & Cook, 1976) have suggested that gazing can also signal affiliation or nurturance. Phrases in English such as "gazing into someone's eyes" or "getting lost in one's eyes" seem to capture this aspect of gaze as well. Fehr and Exline (1987) suggest that the affiliative aspects of gazing may have their roots in infancy, because infants are very attentive, via gaze, to adults, as adults are their source of care and protection.

It is not unusual to think that cultures should come up with rules concerning gazing and visual attention. Both aggression and affiliation are behavioral tendencies that are important for group stability and maintenance. Each culture derives its own set of rules concerning gazing and visual attention to ensure that its members are affiliated while at the same time curbing aggressive tendencies.

Cross-cultural research on gazing in humans has also produced some very interesting findings. Several studies have shown that people from Arabic cultures gaze much longer and more directly at their partners than Americans do (Hall, 1963; Watson & Graves, 1966). Watson (1970) studied visual attention patterns in 30 different countries and separated the countries according to whether they were a "contact" culture (that is, those that facilitated physical touch or contact during interaction) or a "noncontact" culture. Watson found that people in contact cultures engaged in more gazing than did people of noncontact cultures. In addition, people from contact cultures had more direct orientations when interacting with others, less distance, and more touching.

When a person does not look at us as much as we are used to normally when interacting, it seems to be common to all people to make some negative attributions about that behavior. For example, we may believe that the other person is not interested in us or in our conversation. We may believe that the other person does not want to be there or wants to break off the conversation. I have often heard how many Americans get frustrated and perplexed when interacting with people from some Asian cultures, because it seems as if the people from Asian cultures do not look directly at the other person when interacting. We may feel negatively about this person, wondering if they feel angry at us or are not interested romantically or are lying. It is important to keep this in the proper perspective, however. Watson and Hall both mention that many people from Arabic cultures get annoyed when interacting with Americans, probably because the Americans tend to gaze less than the Arabs are used to. This is a two-way street!

Even within the United States, there are differences in gaze and visual behavior between different groups of Americans. A number of studies have shown that African Americans tend to gaze less directly than do European Americans when interacting with someone (Exline, Jones, & Maciorowski, 1977; LaFrance & Mayo, 1976). In studies of interethnic interactions, Fehr (1977, 1981) studied African American and European American mixed and same ethnicity interactions and found that the African Americans gazed less directly, repeating the findings of other researchers. Fehr also found, moreover, that the participants tended to prefer people who gazed at about the same amounts as they were typically accustomed to, regardless of ethnicity.

Studies from nonhuman primates, across human cultures, and within our own culture all indicate that gaze is an important aspect of social and interactive behavior. When we encounter people who gaze differently than we are used to, we often come away from those interactions with negative or questioning feelings about our relationship with the other person or about that person. If the other person does not gaze as much as we are accustomed, we tend to make negative attributions about that person's interest in us or in the conversation. If the other person gazes too much, we feel that person is too aggressive or domineering in some way.

These attributions occur only if we use the rules of interpretation we are accustomed to. If the person with whom we are interacting is from another culture, operating with another set of rules, our interpretations of that gaze behavior may actually be wrong. What if the other person is not looking at you directly out of deference or appreciation for your status or power? Although looking a person straight in the eye has some roots in our American culture, other cultures may not have these roots but still exhibit this behavior more strongly than we do.

Interpersonal Space and Proxemics

Space is another extremely important dimension of nonverbal behavior that we often take for granted. How we use space can send important messages about power, status, and dominance. This is true for people in interactions as well as in their own private spaces. Have you ever noticed how some of the more powerful people in a company or organization seem to have spaces that are the most remote and difficult to access? The people with the most power in an organization usually have the nicest spaces, and certainly some of the largest spaces. Even within a certain floor the people with the most power seem to have the corner spaces, with a view to the outside world and limited access to their space from the inside. People with less power are accessible by everyone from all directions; people with more power are relatively inaccessible.

Like gaze and visual behavior, space is an important nonverbal dimension in animals and nonhuman primates. Animal societies, humans included, seem to come up with rules about how to use space optimally given space restrictions and other limitations placed on them for survival. Hall (1978) reports that deer, gulls, and pelicans have ordered rules about spacing in their colonies. Calhoun (1950) conducted a study with 150 rats and found that the rats seemed to settle "naturally" into 12 groups of approximately 12 rats each, given a certain amount of space in which to live.

The rules we develop in relation to interpersonal spacing are highly dependent on the space resources we have available to us. The rules we develop, in turn, have dramatic effects on the rules of social interaction, appropriateness, and politeness that we must subsequently adopt to survive, given the size of the population and space available for them (population density). These rules form the basis for what become our cultural rules about interpersonal space. Also, these rules feed off the space and population density, which in turn feed off the rules, forming a circular, self-renewing cycle.

Americans, like people from other cultures and countries, have developed rules governing the use of interpersonal space. Hall (1978) specifies four different levels of interpersonal space use depending on social relationship type. The closest type of relationship, intimate relationships, are characterized by interpersonal spaces of between 0 and 1½ feet. Personal relationships are generally characterized by distances of 1½ feet to 4 feet. Social consultive relationships are generally characterized by distances between 4 and 8 to 10 feet. Relationships that involve distances greater than 10 feet are generally considered public relationships.

This is a general guide to interpersonal distances in the United States for Americans, but other cultures will define different distances for these same relationships. Indeed, cross-cultural research on interpersonal distance and space has shown exactly that. Watson and Graves (1966) studied pairs of male students from Arab cultures and compared their use of space against the use of space of similar male pairs of American students. They found that Arab males tended to sit closer to each other, with more direct, confrontational types of body orientations. They had greater eye contact and tended to speak in louder voices than did the Americans. Hall (1963, 1966), in fact, concluded that people from Arab cultures generally learn to interact with others at distances close enough to feel the other person's breath.

Other cross-cultural studies show how people of different cultures learn to use space differently in interpersonal contexts. Forston and Larson (1968) cited anecdotal evidence of how students with Latin American backgrounds tended to interact more closely than did students of European backgrounds. Noesjirwan (1977, 1978) reported that Indonesian subjects tended to sit closer than did the Australian subjects in the studies. Shuter (1977) reported that Italians interacted more closely than did either Germans or Americans. Shuter (1976) also reported that people from Colombia generally interacted at closer distances than did the subjects from Costa Rica.

It is no wonder that we can come away from interpersonal interactions with people of different cultural backgrounds feeling quite negatively about them. For example, if we Americans were to interact with someone from a culture (such as an Arab culture) who learned to interact much more closely than we were accustomed, we would probably be quite put off by this. If this person were a casual acquaintance, we would probably interact with this person at a distance comfortable to us, say, 4 to 5 feet. But, this person may want to get right up to our face and talk. As this happened, we would probably try to back up, adjusting to the closing gap. That person would probably keep coming on. We might feel as if we were being stalked! We may think, "How dare this person talk to me as if he were an intimate friend of mine!" We may leave feeling quite offended, when in fact that person may have just been trying to interact at the distance he has learned is appropriate for your type of relationship.

The opposite can and does occur. For example, a man might want to get closer to someone, trying to gauge whether she has a romantic interest in him. She may be from a culture that dictates more space between people, even in intimate, romantic relationships, than he is accustomed to. She may sit farther from him than he would like, but it actually may be closer to him than is appropriate for her. He would interpret that she doesn't feel anything for him. She, on the other hand, may feel that she is getting too involved!

Differences in the rules we all have concerning the use of space in interpersonal contexts can pose major problems in intercultural communication situations. Like other nonverbal behaviors, our use of space and our interpretation of the use of space around us often happens automatically and unconsciously. We have internalized these unspoken cultural rules and act on them automatically. And just as we operate on them automatically, people from all other cultures do so as well. But their rules may be different from ours, and we need to take these differences into account when understanding and interacting with people of different cultures.

Gestures

Say you met someone in class whom you were attracted to. One day, you worked up enough courage to go up to him or her and ask for a date. You are busy making conversation, kind of fumbling around with your words, hands, and books. Finally, you pop the question—will he or she go out with you tonight? He or she nods. You're about ready to jump through the ceiling with excitement. But you'd better control yourself, you think to yourself, and make arrangements to see him or her later. He or she nods again. You go away calm, cool, and oh so collected. Later that night, you show up to pick up your date, but your date is not there. Your date left word with a roommate that he or she won't be there. What happened?

Well, if your date were an American using an American gesture (head nod), then something would be definitely strange. But if your date were from another culture—where nodding the head means no, and shaking the head means yes—then he or she was telling you no all along! Although people of most cultures seem to nod their heads when meaning yes and shake their heads when meaning no, there are some cultures (for example, some parts of Greece and Turkey) where the people do exactly the opposite (Ekman, Friesen, & Bear, 1984; Kendon, 1987).

Gestures are movements of the body, usually the hands, that are generally reflective of thought or feeling. Like language, gestures are culture-specific and differ in each culture. But when we use them, especially in intercultural contexts, we don't readily think about the fact that they may have a different meaning to someone else. Being unaware of these differences can definitely cause problems. At the very least, you might miss out on some dates.

Many cultures emphasize differences in the use of gestures as illustrators. **Illustrators** are actions that highlight or accent speech or speech content. Some cultures (for example, Jewish, Italian) encourage their members to be very expressive in their gestures and mannerisms when speaking. Other cultures (for example, Japan, Thailand) encourage their members to be more reserved in using gestures as illustrators. It is amazing how we become accustomed to our cultural norms and expectations concerning gestures. In cultures that encourage gestures as illustrators (what Kendon, 1987, would call "gesticulation"), people think nothing of it when interacting with people who seem to flail about, using large hand movements (and hopefully some safe distance!) when talking to others. In fact, people of these cultures would probably think something was wrong when they interact with people from more reserved cultures. Conversely, people from more reserved cultures may think something is strange when they interact with gesturally expressive people. They may actually feel threatened or overwhelmed when interacting with these people.

The possibility of unnecessary intercultural conflict is large. We can come away from intercultural communication situations with quite negative feelings about the people we were interacting with or about the conversation topic. These feelings may generalize into detrimental stereotypes about all people of that culture. All this may occur solely on the basis of cultural differences in gestures, gesticulations, and other nonverbal aspects of communication.

Most cultures have quite an elaborate system of emblematic gestures. **Emblems** are gestures and movements that have a total meaning by themselves. The "finger," thumbs up, A-OK, head nods and shakes, and the V sign are all examples of emblems we use in the United States. Shrugging your shoulders and raising both hands, palms up, is yet another emblematic gesture signaling uncertainty or ignorance about something. We take these emblematic gestures for granted. But there are many stories of travelers from the United States getting into trouble using American gestures in other countries, where the gestures have different meanings. While traveling in some parts of Europe, for example, you don't want to use the A-OK sign. Although you might mean to say that "everything's okay," in some parts of Europe it is a rude or vulgar gesture, often interpreted as an invitation for sex (Ekman et al., 1984). In some other parts of Europe, it might mean that "you're nothing." Pointing your index finger toward your head and temple area in the United States signals that you are smart. In some parts of Europe and Asia, however, it means that you are stupid.

The "V for victory" sign with the index and middle fingers is another example of cultural differences in gestures. This gesture was commonly used in the United States to mean victory, and it has caught on in other countries as well. It is said that some members of the Greek and American military may have insulted former British Prime Minister Winston Churchill when they gave that sign with the palm facing backward instead of forward. Facing backward, it is a common English insult equivalent to our American saying "up yours." The original V for victory sign is signaled with the palm facing outward. But you wouldn't want to do that in Greece, because it is an abbreviated form of an insult in Greece. The gesture evolved in Greece from a practice of people throwing garbage and dirt from the streets toward criminals as they were paraded through the streets.

Japanese often signify that someone is angry by raising the index fingers of both hands, in a pointing fashion, toward the sides of their heads, pointing up. In Brazil and other South American countries, however, this signifies that one wants sex (is horny). Imagine what would happen if a Japanese person were trying to tell someone from Brazil that someone else is angry and the Brazilian interpreted the signal to mean the Japanese person is horny!

These are just a few of the many different types of gestures used around the world, and the differences in their meaning and interpretation. Some scholars have attempted to catalogue in great detail the use of gestures in various different cultures. Many of these resources are in book form (for example, Ekman et al., 1984; Kendon, 1987; Morris, Collett, Marsh, & O'Shaughnessy, 1980), and there is at least one videotape on the market that demonstrates differences in the meaning and use of gestures in different cultures (Archer, 1991).

Conclusion

In this chapter, I have discussed in depth only three types of nonverbal behaviors and how cultures may influence them: gaze and visual attention, interpersonal space and distance, and gestures. There are many other channels and types of nonverbal behaviors. I chose these three areas because of the wealth of cross-cultural research on these topics and because of their impact on the communication process. Indeed, the world of nonverbal behaviors is as complex and varied as that of verbal language. The contribution of nonverbal behavior to the total communication process is no longer debated in the social sciences. This contribution is large indeed.

Unfortunately, despite the degree to which nonverbal behaviors contribute to communication, we often take them for granted. We are so accustomed to sending and receiving nonverbal messages and signals that as adults we do this unconsciously and automatically. We get no formal training on how to send or receive these communications correctly and accurately. We learn spelling, grammar, punctuation, reading, and writing beginning in elementary school, but there is no equivalent formal education system for nonverbal behaviors.

Nonverbal behaviors are just as much a language as any other. Just as verbal languages differ from culture to culture, so do nonverbal languages of each culture. We are all fully aware that verbal languages are different from one culture to the next. That is why we do not hesitate to purchase language reference dictionaries to help us understand different languages.

But in the nonverbal arena, we often take it for granted that our systems of communicating nonverbally are all the same. This is a mistake.

Understanding cultural differences in nonverbal behavior is the first step in the process of truly appreciating cultural differences in communication. To study intercultural communication solely from the standpoint of verbal language will result in the exclusion of an important process of communication.

Can formal training in nonverbal behavior interpretation help intercultural communication processes and outcomes? Although only a few studies on this topic have been published to date, their findings are indeed suggestive of the positive impact of nonverbal skills training. Collett (1971), for example, trained English subjects to engage in more visual attentive types of behaviors when interacting with subjects from Arabic cultures. In later ratings, Arabic subjects preferred interacting with English subjects who had received training over English subjects who had not received training. Yet other English subjects could not discriminate which English people had been trained and which had not. Garratt, Baxter, and Rozelle (1981) trained police officers to engage in gaze and visual attentive behavior patterns that were similar to those found with African Americans in previous studies. The police officers then used these patterns when interviewing male African American undergraduate subjects. The subjects invariably rated the trained officers more favorably than the untrained officers.

These studies do suggest the feasibility and value of training programs in nonverbal behavior. Still, the real task left to those of us who study culture and cultural differences is to recognize the profound influence of nonverbal behaviors on the communication process and then realize how our own cultural background influences the ways we engage and interpret the nonverbal world around us. Although these processes are usually unconscious and automatic, that doesn't mean we can't improve them to be more flexible and inclusive of different cultural systems of behavior. When something occurs within the communication process to "turn you off," take a moment and consider whether there is something cultural that led to your feelings, and if so, go beyond that and try to interpret the underlying intentions within that person's cultural framework. Although not a cure-all for intercultural conflict, this is a good place to start.

Glossary

attention structure   An organized pattern that dictates which animals can look at others, and vice versa. These structures appear to be highly related to dominance hierarchies in animal societies.

emblems   Nonverbal behaviors that convey a message by themselves.

gestures Movements of the body, usually the hands, that are generally reflective of thought or feeling.

illustrators Those nonverbal behaviors used to highlight aspects of the words we speak.

nonverbal behaviors All the behaviors that occur during communication other than words, such as facial expressions; the movements of hands, arms, and legs; posture; characteristics of our voices above and beyond the words we speak; space; gaze; clothing; and so forth.

regulators Nonverbal behaviors we engage in to regulate the flow of speech during a conversation.

Suggested Readings

Ekman, P., & Friesen, W. V. (1969). The repertoire of nonverbal behavior: Categories, origins, usage, and coding. *Semiotica, 1,* 49–98.

Hall, E. T. (1966). *The hidden dimension.* New York: Doubleday.

Culture and Social Behavior

Humans are social animals, and our everyday lives involve many interactions with and influences by others. It is very difficult to think of an existence that is devoid of any contact with others. Our lives, like it or not, are highly enmeshed with those of people around us. For years, social psychologists have studied individual behavior in social context—the way our thoughts, feelings, and behaviors influence, and are influenced by, others. Among the many important topics that fall within the rubric of social psychology are attribution, aggression, altruism, conformity, group productivity, love, and the like.

Of all the areas of interest to psychologists, no area is more influenced by culture than is social psychology. Culture creates the structure by which rules of social behavior and interaction are maintained, thus moderating all psychological processes involving our lives with others. All cultures have different rules regarding the appropriateness of individual behaviors, and these differences are easily evident across the topics studied by cross-cultural, social psychologists. Yet, there are many similarities across cultures as well, especially on the level of underlying intent and goals of behavior.

Because our lives are profoundly influenced by the existence of others, and because culture exerts considerable influence on social behavior, it is important to understand the nature of these cultural influences on social behavior. We need to grasp, on an intellectual as well as behavioral level, how culture interacts with social behavior, so that we can apply the principles of psychology in the most judicious ways to improve our lives. At the same time, understanding how the principles of social psychology may be similar or different across cultural contexts will help develop our critical thinking skills in relation to these topics.

This chapter covers topics related to intergroup behavior; interpersonal attraction and love; conformity, compliance, and obedience; group productivity and social loafing; and person perception and impression formation. Another important topic, attributions or social explanations, was covered in Chapter 2. Because each is a separate topic, each section begins with a brief definition of the topic, describes some of the major findings obtained in research in the United States, and then concludes with findings from cross-cultural research on that topic that may challenge the traditional notions. The chapter ends with a summary of the points in relation to cultural stereotypes and ethnocentrism.

Cultural Differences in Intergroup Behavior

We all live with others, forming attachments, bonds, and relationships. We are close to some people and distant from others. We make friends, acquaintances, and even enemies. Some of the people we see every day we know well, yet other people we see every day we don't know at all. Strangers, family members, friends, co-workers, acquaintances—the list of people in our everyday world is long.

One way social scientists have learned to understand our relationships with different people is by classifying them into categories that approximate the psychological categories we create. Especially important to understanding self-other relationships and pertinent to understanding cultural differences in social behavior is the category of ingroups and outgroups.

Ingroups and Outgroups

The ingroups-outgroups classification is one of the oldest and best-studied social classifications in social psychology and sociology (see Brewer & Kramer, 1985; Messick & Mackie, 1989; and Tajfel, 1982, for reviews and more complete descriptions of this distinction). Most of us intuitively know the difference between ingroups and outgroups. **Ingroup relationships** are relationships characterized by some degree of familiarity, intimacy, and trust. We feel close to the people around us we consider to be in our ingroup. Self-ingroup relationships develop through bonds that tie the ingroup together through common friendships or relationships or goals.

Outgroup relationships are just the opposite. Outgroup relationships lack the familiarity, intimacy, and trust afforded to relationships with ingroup others. Ingroup relationships may be associated with feelings of closeness, but outgroup relationships may lack such feelings altogether and may even involve negative feelings of hostility, aggression, aloofness, or superiority. A bond exists that binds ingroup relationships together, but no such bond exists for our relationships with people on the outside. These people simply exist and are barely in our consciousness. They do not have any special relationship with us.

Although the ingroup-outgroup distinction is dichotomous, we know the world is not that simple. Our social relationships cannot be neatly classified into two categories. There are differing degrees of intimacy, familiarity, and closeness even within one category. Classification schemes like ingroups-outgroups are simply aids that help us understand our behavior with others while acknowledging that greater complexity exists in those relationships.

Much of socialization and enculturation—the time of growing and learning about the rules and standards of our society and culture—is spent learning which people constitute our ingroup and our outgroup. From birth (and arguably before), we are busy building relationships with the people around us. As we go to school, make friends, find jobs, fall in love, and generally go through life, we develop relationships with many different people. Explicitly or implicitly, we categorize those relationships in our own minds according to the dimensions that define our ingroups and outgroups.

The ingroup-outgroup distinction is useful in describing our relationships with others in our culture and is applicable to all cultures and societies of the world. People of all cultures must learn to differentiate among the people they have relationships with. This fact makes this distinction very useful indeed in understanding social behavior around the world and how that social behavior may be influenced by culture.

People of different cultures differ in exactly how these relationships develop, and with whom. The people we generally consider to belong to our ingroup may not be the same people that members of another culture consider to be in their ingroup. The same is true for outgroups. And regardless of whether the same people can be classified as ingroup or outgroup across cultures, the particular shapes, forms, and meanings of those relationships may be entirely different. Understanding and recognizing the existence of ingroup and outgroup relationships and the possibilities for how they may differ forms the basis for understanding how culture can influence these relationships and guide our social behaviors.

Cultural Differences in Ingroup-Outgroup Relationships

Cultural differences in the structure and format of ingroup-outgroup relationships. People of different cultures may not consider the same types of people and relationships when defining ingroups and outgroups. Just because a certain type of person (a friend at school or a work colleague) is an ingroup (or outgroup) member, we cannot assume that people from another culture will interpret and act on those relationships in exactly the same way. And we cannot interpret the relationships of others as we do our own, because they may be entirely different.

Cultures differ in the formation and structure of self-ingroup and self-outgroup relationships in other ways as well. It is not uncommon for ingroup and outgroup membership to change in some cultures as referents to the groups change. This may be particularly difficult for us to understand from our traditional American way of thinking. In our own culture, ingroup and outgroup membership is stable, no matter what we are talking about, to whom we are talking, or where we are talking. Our friends are our friends no matter what, and consistency is an important facet of our psychological makeups. But in another culture, some people may constitute your ingroup in one circumstance or situation but *the same people* may constitute your outgroup in another. It is not uncommon for business-people in Asian cultures, for example, to consider each other outgroups and competitors when talking about domestic business issues. But when the discussion turns to international business, those same outgroup competitors may band together to form an ingroup. This type of switching of ingroup-outgroup relationships is not limited to Asian or collectivistic cultures; it is present in many, if not all, cultures. When former President Bush visited Japan in 1991 with the chief executive officers of many different American companies, they all represented ingroup "Americans," even though those companies and officers would consider each other outgroup rivals in relation to domestic issues. Like many cultural differences, cultures differ in terms of degree but not necessarily presence or absence of this switching phenomenon. That is, the exact depth and meaning of those relationships may differ substantially across cultures.

Cultural differences in the meaning of ingroup-outgroup relationships. Triandis and his colleagues (1988) have done an especially nice job of elucidating how self-ingroup and self-outgroup relationships differ across cultures by using the cultural dimension known as individualism versus collectivism.

Individualism-collectivism (IC) is one of the most important social psychological dimensions of culture. Many writers across the social science disciplines have used this dimension to understand differences in social behaviors across the cultures they have studied (for example, Hofstede, 1980, 1983; Kluckholn & Strodtbeck, 1961; Mead, 1961; Triandis, 1972). IC refers to the degree to which a culture promotes individual needs, wishes, desires, and values over group and collective ones. Individualistic cultures encourage their members to become unique individuals; hierarchical power and status differences are minimized, while equality is emphasized. Collectivistic cultures stress the needs of a group; individuals are identified more through their group affiliation than by individual position or attributes. Hierarchical differences and vertical relationships are emphasized, and role, status, and appropriate behaviors are more clearly defined by position.

Self-ingroup and self-outgroup relationships differ in individualistic and collectivistic cultures. And these differences in the meaning of ingroup and outgroup relationships produce differences in the types of behaviors people engage in when interacting with others. In individualistic cultures, for example, a person may belong to many ingroups, and indeed, many people in individualistic cultures belong to multiple ingroups. In our culture, for instance, which is traditionally quite individualistic, many of us belong to several ingroups—music groups, sport groups, church groups, social groups, and so forth. Children in America today may belong to football teams during football season, basketball teams during basketball season, and baseball teams during baseball season. They may take swimming, piano, or violin lessons, be members of Boy Scouts or Girl Scouts, and generally just be the busiest people around. This is not the case in collectivistic cultures. Members of collectivistic cultures belong to fewer ingroups. People in many Asian and South American cultures do not belong to all the different sports, music, and social groups that people in individualistic cultures like ours do.

This characteristic of individualistic and collectivistic cultural differences in ingroup membership has important consequences to the commitment people have to different groups. In general, in exchange for belonging to fewer groups, people in collectivistic cultures have greater commitments to the groups to which they belong. They also identify more with the groups to which they belong; that is, the groups themselves become an integral part of each individual's self-concept and identity. This makes sense because by definition collectivistic cultures depend on groups to a much greater degree, and subjugating personal goals in favor of collective goals is a necessity.

Members of individualistic cultures do not necessarily collapse their sense of self-identity and self-concept into the groups to which they belong. They have fewer commitments to their ingroups and move much more easily from ingroup to ingroup. Although groups take on special importance in collectivistic cultures, the same degree of importance does not exist for group membership in individualistic cultures.

It follows that collectivistic cultures require a greater degree of harmony, cohesion, and cooperation within their ingroups and place greater burdens on individuals to identify with the group and conform to group norms. Sanctions usually exist for nonconformity. Individualistic cultures, however, depend less on groups and more on the uniqueness of their individuals. The pursuit of personal goals rather than collective ones is of primary importance. As a result, individualistic cultures require less harmony and cohesion within groups and place less importance on conformity of individuals to group norms.

These differences in the meaning of self-ingroup relationships between individualistic and collectivistic cultures have consequences for behavior. In collectivistic cultures, for example, you would expect people to
make more individual sacrifices for their ingroups in pursuit of group
goals. You would expect to see people trying harder to cooperate with
each other, even if it means that the individual must suppress his or her
own feelings, thinking, behaviors, or goals to maintain harmony and cohesion. You would expect people to try to find ways of agreeing with each
other more, downplaying and minimizing interpersonal differences for
the sake of harmony.

Self-ingroup relationships in individualistic cultures have different
consequences for behavior. In these cultures, you would expect people to
make fewer sacrifices of their own individual goals, needs, and desires for
the sake of a common good. You would expect people to be more expressive of their own feelings, attitudes, opinions, without as much fear or
worry about the consequences to group harmony or cohesion. You would
expect people to bring up interpersonal concerns, problems, and conflicts
more freely.

Not only do self-ingroup relationships differ between individualistic
and collectivistic cultures, but self-outgroup relationships also differ. In
collectivistic cultures, the primary focus of attention is on ingroup relationships. For that reason, relationships with outgroup people are marked
by a relative lack of concern. To the degree to which members of collectivistic cultures focus on harmony, cohesion, and cooperation in ingroup relations, distancing, aloofness, and even discrimination with regard to self-
outgroup relationships also exists. The opposite is true in individualistic
cultures. People of individualistic cultures are more likely to treat outgroup persons more equally, with relatively less distinction between ingroups and outgroups. Members of individualistic cultures engage in positive, relationship-building behaviors with outgroup others that members
of collectivistic cultures would reserve only for ingroup others. These concepts are summarized in Table 4.1.

Cultural differences in the meaning of self-ingroup and self-outgroup
relationships have particular meaning for the emotions expressed in social interactions (see Matsumoto, 1991, for an extended discussion). In
general, the familiarity and intimacy of self-ingroup relations in all cultures provide the safety and comfort to express emotions freely along
with tolerance for a broad spectrum of emotional behaviors. Part of emotional socialization involves learning who are ingroup and outgroup
members and the appropriate behaviors associated with them.

Collectivistic cultures foster more positive and fewer negative emotions toward ingroups because ingroup harmony is more important to
them. Positive emotions ensure maintenance of this harmony; negative
emotions threaten it. Likewise, individualistic cultures foster more positive and fewer negative emotions toward outgroups. It is less important in

Table 4.1 Characteristics of Self-Ingroup and Self-Outgroup Relationships in Individualistic and Collectivistic Cultures

	Type of Culture	
	Individualistic	*Collectivistic*
Self-ingroup relations	more emphasis on personal and individual needs, goals, and desires	more emphasis on group goals and maintenance of harmony, cohesion, and cooperation
Self-outgroup relations	more likely to treat them as ingroup members	more likely to make distinctions from in-groups and use distancing and discrimination against them

individualistic cultures to differentiate between ingroups and outgroups, and thus they allow expression of positive feelings and suppression of negative ones toward outgroup members. Collectivistic cultures, however, foster more negative expressions toward outgroups to distinguish more clearly between ingroups and outgroups and to strengthen ingroup relations (via the collective expression of negative feelings toward outgroups). These consequences for personal emotions are summarized in Table 4.2

Table 4.2 Consequences for Personal Emotions in Self-Ingroup and Self-Outgroup Relationships in Individualistic and Collectivistic Cultures

	Type of Culture	
	Individualistic	*Collectivistic*
Self-ingroup relations	okay to express negative feelings; less need to display positive feelings	suppress expressions of negative feelings; more pressure to display positive feelings
Self-outgroup relations	suppress negative feelings; okay to express positive feelings as would toward ingroups	encouraged to express negative feelings; suppress display of positive feelings reserved for ingroups

Interpersonal Attraction and Love

Research on **interpersonal attraction** and love in the United States has produced a number of interesting findings, mainly focusing on the key factors that contribute to attraction. For example, several studies have shown that proximity influences attraction. Early research (for example, Festinger, Schachter, & Back, 1950) showed that people who lived closer to one another were more likely to like one another. Despite the amount of time that has passed since this study, findings from some recent studies still support this notion. In the late 1970s, for instance, Ineichen (1979) showed that people who lived closer together were more likely to get married.

Physical attractiveness has been shown to be quite influential in interpersonal relationships (Patzer, 1985). This attractiveness, however, may be more important for females than for males (Buss, 1988). Although people prefer physically attractive partners in romantic relationships, the **matching hypothesis** suggests that people of approximately equal physical characteristics are likely to select each other as partners. Likewise, the **similarity hypothesis** suggests that people similar in age, race, religion, social class, education, intelligence, attitudes, and physical attractiveness tend to form intimate relationships (Brehm, 1985; Hendrick & Hendrick, 1983). The **reciprocity hypothesis** suggests that people tend to like others who like them.

Among the prevalent theories of love and attachment in American psychology are Hatfield and Berscheid's and Sternberg's. Hatfield and Berscheid's theory proposes that romantic relationships are characterized by two kinds of love (Berscheid & Walster, 1978; Hatfield, 1988). One is **passionate love,** involving an absorption of another that includes sexual feelings and intense emotion. The second is **companionate love,** involving warm, trusting, and tolerant affection for another whose life is deeply intertwined with one's own.

Sternberg's (1988) theory is similar but further divides companionate love into two components: intimacy and commitment. **Intimacy** refers to warmth, closeness, and sharing in a relationship. **Commitment** refers to an intention to maintain a relationship in spite of the difficulties that arise. In Sternberg's theory, eight different forms of love can exist, depending on the presence or absence of each of the three factors. When all three exist, Sternberg calls that relationship **consummate love.**

Attitudes about interpersonal attraction may differ considerably across cultures. Ting-Toomey (1991), for example, compared ratings of love commitment, disclosure maintenance, ambivalence, and conflict expression by 781 subjects from France, Japan, and the United States. Love commitment was measured by ratings of feelings of attachment, belonging, and commitment to the partner and relationship; disclosure maintenance by ratings of feelings concerning private self in the relationship;

ambivalence by ratings of feelings of confusion or uncertainty regarding the partner or the relationship; and conflict expression by ratings of frequency of overt arguments and seriousness of problems. The French and the Americans gave significantly higher ratings than did the Japanese on love commitment and disclosure maintenance. The Americans also gave significantly higher ratings than did the Japanese on relational ambivalence. The Japanese and the Americans, however, had significantly higher ratings than did the French on conflict expression.

Simmons, vomKolke, and Shimizu (1986) examined attitudes toward love and romance among American, German, and Japanese students. The results indicated that romantic love was valued more in the United States and Germany than in Japan. These authors suggested that this cultural difference arose because romantic love is more highly valued in less traditional cultures with few strong, extended-family ties, and less valued in cultures where kinship networks influence and reinforce the relationship between marriage partners.

In another study, Furnham (1984) administered the Rokeach Value Survey to groups of South Africans, Indians, and Europeans. The Europeans valued love more than did the South Africans and the Indians. The South Africans, however, placed higher value on equality and peace.

Despite differences in the definitions and importance of attraction, love, and romance, however, some research suggests that there may be amazing cross-cultural agreement in sex differences with regard to mate selection. The most well-known studies on this topic include that by Buss (1989). In this study, over 10,000 respondents in 37 different cultures drawn from 33 countries completed two questionnaires, one dealing with factors in choosing a mate and the second dealing with preferences concerning potential mates. In 36 of the 37 cultures, females rated financial prospects as more important than did males; in 29 of those 36 cultures, females also rated ambition and industriousness as more important than did males. In all 37 cultures, males preferred younger mates, whereas females preferred older mates; in 34 of the cultures, males rated good looks as more important than did females; and in 23 of the cultures, males rated chastity higher as an important variable in choosing a mate than did females. Buss (1989) concluded that females valued cues related to resource acquisition in potential mates more highly than did males, whereas males valued reproductive capacity more highly than did females. These findings were predicted, in fact, on the basis of an evolutionary-based framework that generated hypotheses related to evolutionary concepts of parental involvement, sexual selection, reproductive capacity, and certainty of paternity or maternity. The degree of agreement in sex differences across cultures has led Buss (1989) and his colleagues to view these mate selection preferences as universal and developed on the basis of different evolutionary selection pressures on males and females.

Conformity, Compliance, and Obedience

Conformity refers to the yielding of people to real or imagined social pressure. **Compliance** is generally defined as the yielding of people to social pressure regarding their public behavior, even though their private beliefs may not have changed. **Obedience** is a form of compliance that occurs when people follow direct commands, usually from someone in a position of authority.

Two of the most well-known studies in American psychology on conformity, compliance, and obedience are the Asch and Milgram studies. Asch's studies (1951, 1955, 1956) examined subjects' responses to a simple judgment task when experimental confederates responding before the subject all give the incorrect response. Across studies and trials, group size and group unanimity were major influencing factors. Conformity would peak when the groups included seven people and the group was unanimous in their judgments (even though the judgments were clearly wrong). Compliance in Asch's studies resulted from subtle, implied pressure. But in the real world, compliance can occur in response to explicit rules, requests, and commands.

In Milgram's studies (1963, 1964, 1974), subjects were brought into a laboratory presumably to study the effects of punishment on learning. Subjects were instructed to provide shocks to another subject (actually an experimental confederate) when the latter gave the wrong response or no response. The apparent shock meter was labeled from "slight shock" to "DANGER: Severe Shock," and the confederate's behaviors ranged from simple utterances of pain through pounding on the walls, pleas to stop, and then deathly silence. Despite these conditions, 65% of the subjects obeyed the commands of the experimenter and administered the most severe levels of shock.

To this day, these studies stand as premier examples in American psychology of the potentially harmful and negative consequences of conformity and obedience. Many cross-cultural studies, however, particularly with Asian cultures, indicate that not only do people of other cultures engage in conforming, compliant, and obedient behaviors to a greater degree than do Americans, but that they also value conformity to a greater degree. For example, Punetha, Giles, and Young (1987) administered an extended Rokeach Value Survey to three groups of Asian subjects and a group of British subjects. The British clearly valued individualistic items, such as independence and freedom, whereas the Asian subjects endorsed societal values including conformity and obedience.

Studies involving other Asian versus American comparisons have generally produced the same results. Hadiyono and Hahn (1985), for example, showed that Indonesians endorsed conformity more than did Americans. Argyle, Henderson, Bond, Iizuka, and Contarello (1986) showed that the

Japanese and Hong Kong Chinese endorsed obedience more than did British and Italian subjects. Buck, Newton, and Muramatsu (1984) showed that the Japanese were more conforming than were Americans.

Some studies have shown that these differences are not limited to Asian cultures. Cashmore and Goodnow (1986), for example, demonstrated that Italians were more conforming than Anglo-Australians. El-Islam (1983) documented cultural differences in conformity in an Arabian sample.

These findings are undoubtedly related to cultural differences in values regarding individualism versus collectivism. Traditional American culture fosters individualistic values, thus endorsing behaviors and beliefs contrary to conformity. To conform in American culture is to be weak or deficient somehow. But this is not true in other cultures. Many cultures foster more collective, group-oriented values, and concepts of conformity, obedience, and compliance enjoy much higher status and positive orientation than in the United States. In these cultures, conformity is not only viewed as "good," it is necessary for the successful functioning of the culture, its groups, and the interpersonal relationships of the members of that culture.

Cross-cultural studies on child-rearing values speak to the strength of these values in socialization. Two studies have shown that not only Asians but also Puerto Rican subjects value conformity and obedience as child-rearing values (Burgos & Diaz-Perez, 1986; Stropes-Roe & Cochrane, 1990). A number of anthropological works on the Japanese culture (for example, Benedict, 1946; K. Doi, 1985) indicate the importance of obedience and compliance in child-rearing in that culture.

Group Behavior: Productivity versus Social Loafing

Research on group behavior has received considerable attention in the literature, covering such topics as the bystander effect and altruistic behaviors, group decision-making processes, and productivity. Each of these areas affects real-life settings and issues and forms the basis for many intervention techniques, especially in organizational and industrial psychology. One well-known area of study in this field is on group productivity.

Research on group productivity has typically shown that individual productivity often declines in larger groups (Latane, Williams, & Harkins, 1979). These findings have contributed to the coining of the term, **social loafing**. Two factors appear to contribute to this phenomenon. One is the reduced efficiency resulting from the loss of coordination among workers' efforts. As group membership increases, presumably the lack of coordination among the people tends to reduce efficiency, resulting in lack of activity or duplicate activity. This consequently results in loss of productivity.

The second factor typically identified as a contributor to lack of group productivity involves the reduction in effort by individuals when they work in groups as compared to when they work by themselves. Latane and his colleagues (Latane, 1981; Latane, Williams, & Harkins, 1979) have conducted a number of studies investigating group size, coordination, and effort. They have found that larger groups produced lack of both co-ordination and effort, resulting in decreased productivity. Latane (1981) attributed these findings to a diffusion of responsibility in groups. That is, as group size increases, the responsibility for getting a job done is divided among more people, and many group members slack off because their individual contribution is less recognizable.

Several cross-cultural studies, however, suggest that social loafing is *not* generalizable across other cultures. Earley (1989), for example, examined social loafing in an organizational setting among managerial trainees in the United States and the People's Republic of China. Subjects in both cultures worked on a task under conditions of low or high accountability and low or high shared responsibility. The results were clear, indicating that social loafing was observed only among the American subjects, whose individual performances in a group were less than when working alone, but not among the Chinese.

Shirakashi (1985) and Yamaguchi, Okamoto, and Oka (1985) conducted studies involving Japanese participants in several tasks. They showed that not only did social loafing not occur, but exactly the opposite occurred. That is, being in a group enhanced individual performance of their subjects rather than diminished it. Gabrenya, Wang, and Latane (1985) also demonstrated this **social striving** in a sample of Chinese schoolchildren.

Explanations for social striving in other cultures have centered on the culture's degree of collectivism. Collectivistic cultures such as China and Japan foster interpersonal interdependence and group collective functioning more than does the individualistic American culture. As a result, groups tend to be more productive in these cultures, precisely because they foster coordination among ingroup members. They also place higher value on individual contributions in group settings.

Interestingly, several studies involving American subjects have begun to challenge the traditional notions of social loafing (for example, Harkins, 1987; Harkins & Petty, 1982; Shepperd & Wright, 1989; Weldon & Gargano, 1988; Zaccaro, 1984). Jackson and Williams (1985), for instance, showed that Americans working collectively indeed improved performance and productivity. Thus, our notions of social loafing and group productivity are challenged not only cross-culturally but within our own American culture as well. With increased American interest in the organizational and management styles of other countries, particularly Japan, this topic is sure to gain even more attention in the future.

Person Perception and Impression Formation

This area is important in social psychology because psychologists have long realized the influence of impressions and perceptions of others in our interactions and dealings with them. Questions concerning the degree to which impressions influence our actual behaviors, and the extent to which people's expectations color their impressions of others, fall within the purview of **person perception**. Psychologists are also concerned with questions concerning whether bad first impressions can be overcome.

Research in the United States has shown that appearance, especially physical attractiveness, influences judgments of personality. In general, people tend to ascribe desirable personality characteristics to those who are good looking, seeing them as more sensitive, kind, sociable, pleasant, likable, and interesting than those who are unattractive (Dion, 1986; Patzer, 1985). Attractive people are also judged as more competent and intelligent (Ross & Ferris, 1981).

Other aspects of appearance also influence our perceptions of others. For example, greater height has been associated with perceptions of leadership ability, competence, and salary (Deck, 1968; Patzer, 1985). Adults with baby-face features tend to be judged as more warm, kind, naive, and submissive; adults with more mature facial features tend to be judged as strong, worldly, and dominant (Berry & McArthur, 1985, 1986). People who are neat dressers are thought to be conscientious (Albright, Kenny, & Malloy, 1988). People with poor eye contact are often judged as dishonest (DePaulo, Stone, & Lassiter, 1985).

Research on person perception in the United States has also focused on the ways in which impressions are formed and information about others is stored. Much attention has been given to the study of cognitive or social schemas as organizational tools. **Social schemas** are organized clusters of ideas about categories of social events and people and have been shown to widely influence person perceptions (Zajonc, 1985). Much attention has also been given to the study of stereotypes and their influence on our impressions of others. **Stereotypes** are widely held beliefs that people have certain characteristics because of their membership in a particular group. Finally, social psychologists have studied the influence of *selectivity* of our perceptions of others to either confirm or disconfirm beliefs and stereotypes.

Many cross-cultural studies, however, challenge our traditional notions of person perception in American psychology. For example, cross-cultural studies of nonverbal behavior—including gaze, proximity, touching behaviors, verbal utterances, and facial expressions—all speak to the impact of culture on communication. Differences in these behaviors arising from differences in cultural upbringing undoubtedly affect our perception of people of different cultures. We are often unaware of the existence of cultural differences or are unprepared to deal with them. Thus, it is easy to form negative perceptions of others because of cultural differences in these nonverbal behaviors.

Although the effects of attractiveness and physical appearance on the formation of positive impressions are well documented, cultures clearly differ on the meaning and definition of attractiveness. Beauty can be a quite relative judgment, and people of different cultures can have quite different, and distinct, concepts of what is beautiful and what is not. Cultural differences in the definition of attractiveness can clearly affect its influence on the formation of impressions.

Cultural differences in facial expressions also speak to the impact of cultures on person perception. In one study (Matsumoto & Kudoh, 1993), for example, American and Japanese subjects were asked to judge Caucasian and Japanese faces that were either smiling or neutral on three dimensions: attractiveness, intelligence, and sociability. The Americans consistently rated the smiling faces higher on all three dimensions, congruent with our traditional notions of person perception and impression formation. The Japanese, however, rated the smiling faces only as more sociable. There was no difference in their ratings of attractiveness between smiling and neutral expressions, and they rated the neutral faces as more intelligent.

Even when different cultures agree on overall dimensional judgments of others, they may disagree on what kinds of behavioral consequences those judgments may have. For example, Bond and Forgas (1984) presented Chinese and Australian subjects with a description of a target person varying across dimensions such as extroversion, agreeableness, conscientiousness, and emotional stability. Across both cultures, target-person conscientiousness was linked with intentions of trust, whereas extroversion and agreeableness were linked to intentions of association. However, the Chinese subjects were much more likely than were the Australians to form behavioral intentions of trust and to form behavioral associations based on agreeableness.

Conclusion: Cultures, Stereotypes, and Ethnocentrism

Improving our understanding of the dynamics of person perception and its influence on the development and maintenance of stereotypes is extremely important in today's world. Despite the steps that we have taken to close the gap between different groups of people in the last few decades, especially between the races, the 1992 riots in Los Angeles and the cries to "Buy American!" in the last few years both testify to the pervasive and strong sentiments of "groupism" that can have negative, and positive, effects.

As discussed throughout this book, culture influences behavior, thoughts, and feelings and produces differences that challenge our preconceived notion of psychology in the United States. These differences are especially applicable to the area of person perception. Cultural differences in behaviors can lead to misperceptions, and misjudgments, of people.

The first way in which cross-cultural psychology impacts on our knowledge and understanding of person perception and intergroup relationships is by improving our understanding of "culture." Most cross-cultural psychologists would agree that culture is a sociopsychological phenomenon—the shared attitudes, beliefs, values, and behaviors communicated from one generation to the next via language (Barnouw, 1985). This definition of culture is "fuzzy," not clear, and soft, not hard. Culture is *not* race per se, although a race in general may embrace a particular culture. Culture is *not* nation per se, although people of different nations in general embrace their own cultures. In this light, many of the behaviors we observe in people of other races or nations seem different because of differences in culture, not necessarily differences in race or nationality.

Ironically, however, it is precisely these cultural differences in behavior that give rise to stereotypes. We often observe people of different races engaging in behavior that we may not deem appropriate or acceptable given a certain situation or context. Many times we interpret these behaviors within *our own* cultural background and upbringing, and *attribute* those behaviors to reasons that make sense only within our own cultural understanding. We may do this automatically, without pause or consideration of the different cultural backgrounds or circumstances that may have brought about the behavior in the first place. This type of nonrecognition of a cultural viewpoint other than our own may lay the foundation for *ethnocentrism*—the tendency to interpret the behaviors and events around us through our own cultural filter. We may become selective in the events that we perceive and in the attributions that we assign to them.

Improving our understanding of culture, however, helps us to bridge the gap between groups and to begin to break away from the bonds of ethnocentrism. By recognizing that culture is neither race nor nation, we can begin to break persistent racial stereotypes and to search for cultural—that is, sociopsychological—reasons for differences in behavior. At the same time, we need to search our own culture to find reasons these stereotypes have persisted and how our own culture may be fostered or facilitated by their maintenance.

Cross-cultural psychology also informs us about *variability* within groups and cultures. No single score on any scale can describe or define a culture in its broadest sense. Culture is much too grand and rich to be defined by one component. Culture is not the *average* across a set of people; all the people, their diversity as well as their homogeneity, contribute to that culture. Improving our understanding of the great diversity and variability that exists within any culture will help to release us from stereotypes that we may carry in our interactions with people of different cultures. By recognizing that this degree of diversity exists in all cultures, we are free to allow ourselves to engage with people on their grounds, rather than by predetermining their actions, behaviors, and reasons via stereotype.

Finally, cross-cultural psychology informs us about the importance of cultural background, upbringing, and heritage and their impact on our present-day behaviors. Many of our behaviors as adults are not only shaped by culture, but also draw their meaning from culture. Recognizing the important contributions of culture to behaviors and reasons for these behaviors helps us to understand, respect, and appreciate the differences when we observe them in real life.

Glossary

commitment   An intention to maintain a relationship in spite of the difficulties that arise.

companionate love   Love characterized by warm, trusting, and tolerant affection for another whose life is deeply intertwined with one's own.

compliance   The yielding of people to social pressure in their public behavior, even though their private beliefs may not have changed.

conformity   The yielding of people to real or imagined social pressure.

consummate love   In Sternberg's theory of love, this type of love is characterized by the existence of passionate love, intimacy, and commitment.

ingroup relationships   Relationships characterized by some degree of familiarity, intimacy, and trust. We feel close to people around us we consider to be in our ingroup. Self-ingroup relationships develop through bonds that tie the ingroup together through common friendship or relationships or goals.

interpersonal attraction   Positive feelings toward others.

intimacy   Warmth, closeness, and sharing in a relationship.

matching hypothesis   The hypothesis about interpersonal attraction that suggests that people of approximately equal physical characteristics are likely to select each other as partners.

obedience   A form of compliance that occurs when people follow direct commands, usually from someone in a position of authority.

outgroup relationships   Relationships that lack the familiarity, intimacy, and trust afforded to relationships with ingroup others.

passionate love   Love characterized by an absorption of another that includes sexual feelings and intense emotion.

person perception   The process of forming impressions of others.

reciprocity hypothesis   The hypothesis about interpersonal attraction that suggests that people tend to like others who like them.

similarity hypothesis   The hypothesis about interpersonal attraction that suggests that people similar in age, race, religion, social class, education, intelligence, attitudes, and physical attractiveness tend to form intimate relationships.

social loafing   A term coined to describe findings that suggest that individual productivity often declines in larger groups.

social schemas   Organized clusters of ideas about categories of social events and people.

social striving   A term coined to describe findings from cross-cultural research that suggest that being in a group enhances individual performance rather than diminishes it.

stereotypes   Widely held beliefs that people have certain characteristics because of their membership in a particular group.

Suggested Readings

Asante, M., & Gudykunst, W. (1989). *Handbook of intercultural and international communication.* Newbury Park, CA: Sage.

Bond, M. H. (1988). *The cross-cultural challenge to social psychology.* Newbury Park, CA: Sage.

Ferrante, J. (1992). *Sociology: A global perspective.* Belmont, CA: Wadsworth.

Worchel, S., & Austin, W. G. (1986). *Psychology of intergroup relations.* Chicago: Nelson Hall.

5

Culture and Gender

As with so many other aspects of our lives, culture influences all of us in the behaviors associated with being male or female. In the last 20 or 30 years, we have witnessed many changes in the behaviors Americans consider appropriate for males and females. Certainly, American culture is one of the most dynamic in the exploration of sex and gender differences (or similarities). This dynamism has led to a great deal of confusion and conflict, but it has also produced excitement about the changing nature of human relations and culture itself.

Although similar changes may be occurring in other cultures, these changes may not be as decisive or as drastic as is the case in American culture. Differences across cultures in the rate of change in appropriate sex or gender roles and behaviors can easily lead to a negative view of those cultures. I have heard many American students and other adults give negative opinions of gender role differentiation in cultures they thought were old-fashioned or dated. It is important to keep in mind that differences between the sexes exist for a reason, and often those reasons are peculiar to those cultures. We must exercise considerable caution when evaluating other cultures, especially when we do so according to our own standards.

This chapter will examine how culture influences behaviors related to **sex** and **gender** and to what degree psychological or behavioral differences between the sexes are found across cultures. Inevitably, we will find similarities and variability in sex differences across cultures, and recognition of these should help us better understand the role of culture in the production of these similarities and differences. Improvements in our understanding of the influence of culture not only sharpen our critical thinking skills, they also give us more accurate information about the psychological principles that may be of use to us in our psychological adjustment and the betterment of our lives.

A Special Note about the Relationship between Studies of Gender and Culture in Psychology

The study of culture in psychology owes a lot to the study of sex and gender differences, and vice versa. Beginning 20 or 30 years ago, what is commonly known as the women's movement in the United States helped American academic communities evaluate the treatment and presentation of women in textbooks and research. Many people concluded that most research was conducted using men as subjects, and thus most information presented about "people" in academic textbooks and university courses was based on information gathered from men. This bias with regard to gender differences also existed with regard to what scholars considered important to study, the relative status of different studies and topics, and the probability and outlet for publication. Of course, information presented about people gathered from this biased sample would naturally not be entirely generalizable to everyone, given that there are many differences (as well as similarities) between men and women in their needs, concerns, wishes, and behaviors. Scholars, researchers, teachers, and students alike began to question what was presented to them as knowledge about people in general.

In the past several decades, we have come a long way toward improving our knowledge about both men and women in the social sciences. Although questioning the imbalance of research on both men and women was difficult, many behavioral and social scientists have responded well to this inequity in our knowledge and practice. Today, studies of gender differences are commonplace in social science research, and textbooks incorporate sex and gender differences as a standard practice when imparting knowledge about people (although the degree to which the presentation of such material is comparable to the message it should provide is still questioned and debated).

We have been witness to the same type of question with regard to culture. Just as knowledge about women and women's concerns was missing from research and scholarship 30 years ago, knowledge about cultural similarities and differences and cultural diversity had also been missing. Much of this gap still exists today. Many of the same questions are still being raised concerning whether what we are learning in classes and in our laboratories is indeed true for people of all cultures and ethnicities. The answer so far has been "not necessarily." To address this gap, many researchers have made a conscious effort to study behaviors across cultures to learn what is similar across cultures and what is different. The importance we place on the study of both culture and gender today owes much of its impetus to similar concerns with regard to the limitations and boundaries of the information and knowledge we have in psychology.

Cultural Similarities and Differences in Ascribed Gender Roles and Stereotypes

The number of roles available to males and females is limitless. Some cultures foster a certain gender distinction; other cultures foster other distinctions. We are all familiar with traditional **gender role** differentiations—the notion that males should be independent, self-reliant, strong, and emotionally detached, whereas women should be dependent, reliant, weak, nurturant, and emotional. To what degree is this an American or Western cultural phenomenon?

The best-known study of **gender stereotypes** across cultures is one conducted by Williams and Best (1982). These researchers sampled people in 30 countries, involving almost 3000 individuals with between 52 and 120 respondents per country (Williams & Best, 1982). The study was quite simple and involved the use of a questionnaire known as the Adjective Check List (ACL). The ACL is a list of 300 adjectives. Respondents in each country were asked to decide whether each adjective was more descriptive of a male or of a female. Whether the subjects agreed with the assignment of an adjective to males or females was irrelevant; instead, subjects were asked merely to report the characteristics generally associated with males and females in their culture.

The researchers tallied the data from all individuals. Looking at responses within each culture, Williams and Best (1982) established the criterion that if more than two-thirds of a sample from a country agreed on a particular term for either males or females, there was a consensus within that culture for that general characteristic. Then, looking at responses across the cultures, the researchers decided that if two-thirds of the cultures reached a consensus on the characteristic, there was a cross-cultural consensus on that characteristic to describe males and females. These analyses indicated that there was a high degree of pancultural agreement across all the studied countries in the characteristics associated with men and women. Table 5.1 gives 100 items of the pancultural adjective checklist that Williams and Best (1994) reported for men and women.

The degree of consensus these adjectives received in describing males and females is amazing. In fact, Berry, Poortinga, Segall, and Dasen (1992) suggested that "this degree of consensus is so large that it may be appro-

Table 5.1 The 100 Items of the Pancultural Adjective Checklist

Male-Associated		Female-Associated	
Active	Loud	Affected	Modest
Adventurous	Obnoxious	Affectionate	Nervous
Aggressive	Opinionated	Appreciative	Patient
Arrogant	Opportunistic	Cautious	Pleasant
Autocratic	Pleasure-seeking	Changeable	Prudish
Bossy	Precise	Charming	Self-pitying
Capable	Progressive	Complaining	Sensitive
Conceited	Rational	Confused	Sexy
Confident	Realistic	Curious	Shy
Courageous	Reckless	Dependent	Softhearted
Cruel	Resourceful	Dreamy	Sophisticated
Cynical	Rigid	Emotional	Submissive
Determined	Robust	Excitable	Suggestible
Disorderly	Serious	Fault-finding	Talkative
Enterprising	Sharp-witted	Fearful	Timid
Greedy	Show-off	Fickle	Touchy
Hardheaded	Steady	Foolish	Unambitious
Humorous	Stern	Forgiving	Unintelligent
Indifferent	Stingy	Frivolous	Unstable
Individualistic	Stolid	Fussy	Warm
Initiative	Tough	Gentle	Weak
Interests wide	Unfriendly	Imaginative	Worrying
Inventive	Unscrupulous	Kind	Understanding
Lazy	Witty	Mild	Superstitious

Source: "Cross-Cultural Views of Women and Men," by J. E. Williams and D. L. Best. In W. J. Lonner & R. Malpass (Eds.), *Psychology and Culture,* p. 193. Copyright © 1994 Allyn & Bacon. Reprinted by permission.

priate to suggest that the researchers have found a psychological universal when it comes to gender stereotypes" (p. 60). However, Berry et al. (1992) themselves cautioned against making such sweeping generalizations of the data. But the possibility of a universally accepted gender stereotype has interesting ramifications for possible evolutionary similarities across cultures in division of labor between males and females and the psychological characteristics that result from that universal division of labor.

Williams and Best (1982) conducted a second type of analysis on their data in order to summarize their major findings. They scored the adjectives in each country in terms of favorability, strength, and activity to examine how the adjectives were distributed according to affective or emotional meaning. There was surprising congruence in these analyses; the characteristics associated with men were stronger and more active than those associated with women across all countries. On favorability, however, there were cultural differences, with some countries (such as Japan and South Africa) rating the male characteristics more favorable than female, whereas the female characteristics were more favorable in other countries (for example, Italy and Peru).

How are we to interpret these results? It could be that a division of labor for males and females according to reproductive processes produced differences in behaviors that, in turn, produced differences in psychological characteristics. It may be that these psychological characteristics had some evolutionary and adaptive advantages for males and females to fulfill their roles as prescribed by the division of labor. It could be that men and women in all cultures became locked into these set ways, accounting for universal consensus on these descriptors. It could be that men and women become locked into a particular mindset about cultural differences because of perceived social inequality or social forces and indirect communication via mass media and the like. Or these findings could all be a function of the way the research was conducted, using university students as samples in the cultures, which would tend to make the entire sample from the entire experiment more homogeneous than if people were randomly sampled from each culture.

Although it is impossible to disentangle these factors from each other to better interpret the findings, it is important to note that Williams and Best themselves collected and analyzed data concerning gender stereotypes from young children and found a considerable degree of agreement between the findings for children and those for university students (Williams & Best, 1990). This would argue against the notion that the original findings were obtained because of a homogeneity in the samples due to selecting university students (but it would not completely eliminate such an argument).

In a follow-up study, Williams and Best (1990) studied judgments about what males and females should be like, what they should do, and so forth. These are not necessarily judgments of gender roles or stereotypes per se; rather, they are judgments of **gender role ideology**. In conducting this study, Williams and Best asked subjects in 14 countries to complete the ACL in relation to what they believe they are, and what they would like to be. The subjects also completed a sex role ideology scale that generated scores between two polar opposites, labeled "traditional" and "egalitarian." The traditional scores tended to describe gender roles that met with the traditional or universal norms found in their earlier research. Egalitarian scores, in contrast, reflected a tendency for less differentiation between males and females on the various psychological characteristics.

The most egalitarian scores were found in the Netherlands, Germany, and Finland; the most traditional ideologies were found in Nigeria, Pakistan, and India. Women tended to have more egalitarian views than the men. Gender differences within each country, however, were relatively small compared to cross-country differences, which were considerable. In particular, countries with relatively high socioeconomic development, a high proportion of Protestant Christians, a low proportion of Muslims, a high percentage of women employed outside the home, a high proportion of women enrolled in universities, and a greater degree of individualism were associated with more egalitarian scores. These findings make sense, as greater affluence and individualistic tendencies tend to produce a culture that allows women increased access to jobs and education, thus blending traditional gender roles.

In addition to studying gender stereotypes and ideologies, Williams and Best (1990) also examined gender differences in self-concept. The same students in the 14 countries described above rated each of the 300 adjectives of the ACL according to whether the adjectives were descriptive of themselves or their ideal self. Responses were scored according to masculinity/femininity as well as in terms of favorability, strength, and activity. When scored according to masculinity/femininity, both self and ideal-self ratings for men were more masculine than were women's ratings, and vice versa, across all countries. However, both men and women in all countries rated the ideal self as more masculine than their self. In effect, they were saying that they wanted to have more traits traditionally associated with males.

When scored according to the three emotional dimensions, male self-concepts tended to be rated stronger than female self-concepts. Moreover, in some countries, the ratings on the three dimensions were relatively similar between men and women, whereas in other countries the ratings were quite divergent. The degree of differentiation among the ratings themselves may be related to other variables; Williams and Best (1990) suggest that such variables may include socioeconomic status, religion, proportion of women employed outside the home, and the like.

Taken as a whole, these studies suggest there is considerable, perhaps even universal, consensus among cultures in terms of what kinds of psychological characteristics describe males and females. But despite these similarities, there are considerable cultural differences in the degree to which each culture believes in these differentiations as an ideal. It may very well be that attitudes and values about gender appropriate roles are changing too fast in today's world and that research findings must be limited to generalizations about the time frame in which the data were collected. Still, it is interesting that there is a discrepancy between what some cultures believe is the ideal and the degree of consensus that exists concerning what is currently true.

Other Psychological Gender Differences across Cultures

Culture, biology, gender roles, and gender role ideology all interact to produce differences between the genders on a variety of psychological and behavioral outcomes. That is, the division of labor and actual behaviors males and females engage in as a result of their biological and physiological differences help to produce a different psychology or mindset as well. These psychological differences between genders can be considered a product of the differences between males and females because of the division of labor and behaviors surrounding reproduction.

Just as there will be psychological differences between males and females in any one culture, psychological differences can also be found across cultures. And the degree, direction, or exact nature of those gender differences may differ across cultures. That is, whereas one culture may foster a certain type of gender difference, another culture may not foster that difference to the same degree. A third culture may foster that difference even more than the first two cultures. Psychological gender differences across cultures are not simply products of biology and culture; they are also important reinforcers of culture, feeding back onto the culture, behaviors, gender roles, and gender role ideologies. In this cyclical fashion, the psychological products of gender differentiation also become a crucial aspect of the culture-behavior-psychology link that exists among a people and their rituals, traditions, and behaviors.

When the cross-cultural literature on psychological differences between the genders is examined, three general areas of difference stand out: perceptual/spatial/cognitive abilities, conformity and obedience, and aggressiveness (Berry et al., 1992). Studies in each of these areas do indeed show that although there is a general difference between genders, the degree of these differences is indeed different across cultures.

Perceptual/Spatial/Cognitive Abilities

At least in American society, it is common folklore that males are better at mathematical and spatial reasoning tasks, whereas females are better at verbal comprehension tasks. An analysis of the scores for males and females on standardized tests in elementary school, college entrance examinations, or graduate school entrance examinations shows some degree of support for these notions, although the difference between males and females seems to have narrowed in recent years. In their review of the literature, Maccoby and Jacklin (1974) also concluded that males tend to do better on spatial tasks and other tasks having a spatial component. Years ago, however, Berry (1966) pointed out that such differences do not appear to exist among males and females of the Inuit culture in Canada.

That is, neither males nor females were superior on spatial related tasks. Berry suggested that the gender difference did not exist because "spatial abilities are highly adaptive for both males and females in Inuit society, and both boys and girls have ample training and experience that promote the acquisition of spatial ability" (Berry et al., 1992, p. 65).

Following up on the possibility of cultural differences on this gender difference, Berry (1976) and his colleagues conducted a study in which a block design task was given to males and females in 17 different cultures. A stimulus card depicting a geometric representation of a set of blocks was presented, and the task was to manipulate an actual set of blocks to emulate the design provided. The results were interesting and provocative. Although there were indeed several cultures in which males did better than females on the task, there also were several cultures where females did better than males. In interpreting these data, Berry et al. (1992) suggested that male superiority on the task tended to be found in cultures that were tight (that is, relatively homogeneous), sedentary, and agriculturally based, but that female superiority was found in cultures that were loose, nomadic, and hunting-gathering based. In these latter cultures, the roles ascribed to males and females are relatively flexible, as more members perform a variety of tasks related to the survival of the group.

A similar finding was reported in a meta-analysis of the research literature by Born, Bleichrodt, and Van der Flier (1987). These researchers also reported that although no gender differences in overall intelligence were found, gender differences on various subtests of intelligence did occur. Although their findings leave open the question of the exact role of culture on the gender difference, they do show that the differences in the cognitive test scores between males and females are variable across cultures.

Conformity and Obedience

One of the most common gender role stereotypes is that females are more conforming and obedient than are males. This stereotype is no doubt related to the traditional gender roles females and males have acquired, with males traditionally being "head of the household" and making primary decisions over big-ticket items that involve the family. In this traditional viewpoint, females were not to be concerned with such authority and decision-making power; rather, the female role focused on caring for the children and managing the household affairs. In short, females were expected to conform to decisions imposed upon them by males or by society in general.

The degree to which this difference is enacted varies considerably from culture to culture. In Berry's (1976) study, the researchers also obtained an index of the degree to which each person conforms in the 17 cultures included in the sample. Across the 17 cultures, clear variations emerged, and these appeared to be related to the cultural concept of tightness and agriculture reported above for gender differences in spatial reasoning. That is, cultures that were tighter appeared to foster a greater gender difference on conformity, with females being more conformist than males. Tight cultures may require a greater degree of conformity on the part of both males and females to traditional gender roles. In contrast, cultures that were looser fostered less gender difference on conformity, and in some of these cultures, males were found to be more conforming than females. Although traditional gender stereotypes of females being more conforming than males appears to have some validity, considerable cross-cultural difference exists in the degree, and in some cases the direction, of this difference.

Aggressiveness

Another common gender stereotype is that males are more aggressive than females. Indeed, there is support for this stereotype in all cultures for which documentation exists (Block, 1983; Brislin, 1993). Males account for a disproportionate amount of violent crime in both industrialized and nonindustrialized societies. The focus in research on this topic has been adolescent males. Several researchers have searched for the biological correlates of aggression. In particular, some researchers have questioned whether increased levels of the hormone testosterone during male adolescence may account for or contribute to increased aggression in males. Increased testosterone levels have been associated with dominance hierarchies in some nonhuman primates, but the human analog is not as clear. On the basis of the evidence available, it appears that hormones may contribute to some degree of aggressiveness, but culture and the environment can certainly act to encourage or discourage its emergence (Berry et al., 1992).

A study by Barry, Josephson, Lauer, and Marshall (1976) is also interesting with regard to aggressiveness. Given that a biological explanation may not be available for aggression, these researchers examined the degree to which cultures foster aggressive tendencies in the socialization of their children. These researchers found a sex-related difference in the degree of teaching about aggressiveness on average across 150 different cultures. Inspection of their data, however, reveals that this average difference is produced by a disproportionate number of high-scoring cultures in which teaching aggression actually occurs. In fact, a large majority of societies did not show a sex-related difference in teaching aggression.

Thus, neither biology nor sex differences in teaching aggressive acts can account for gender differences in aggression observed across cultures. Some researchers (Berry et al., 1992; Segall, Dasen, Berry, & Poortinga, 1990) offer yet another interesting possibility to explain gender differences in aggression across cultures. They suggest that male aggression may be a compensatory mechanism to offset the conflict produced by a young male's identification with a female care provider and his initiation into adulthood as a male. In this model, aggressiveness is viewed as "gender marking" behavior.

Regardless of the actual mechanism that produces gender differences in aggression across cultures, the evidence is clear: although the gender stereotype of aggressiveness may be generally true, considerable differences exist across cultures as well. What is true for one culture may definitely not be true for another.

Ethnicity and Gender

One of the most pressing issues and concerns facing us in the United States today has to do with gender differences across different ethnicities. Just as people in different cultures in different countries and in faraway lands may have different gender roles and expectations, people of different ethnic backgrounds here in the United States have different gender role expectations as well. Many of these gender differences across ethnic lines are rooted in the cultures people of these ethnicities brought with them when they originally came to the United States. But gender differences we observe in the United States today definitely reflect an "American" influence, making gender issues unique in this culture.

There is really very little research on gender differences between African American males and females. The research that exists typically compares African American males and females to European American males and females (which in itself may be a statement about the nature and politics of studying gender, race, and culture in the United States), and the results convey a flavor of the unique differences, struggles, and strengths of African American males and females. African American males are more likely than European American males to live below the poverty line, die at an early age, make less money, be put in jail, and be executed for a crime. With regard to psychological processes, African American males are especially adept at body language and nonverbal encoding and decoding and improvised problem solving (Allen & Santrock, 1993).

Research on the concerns of African American females suggests a changing picture over the last 20 years (Hall, Evans, & Selice, 1989). Early research focused almost exclusively on generally negative characteristics and situations. Of late, however, an increasing amount of research has focused on many other psychological aspects of African American females, including self-esteem or achievement. For example, the number of Ph.Ds awarded to African American women increased by 16% between 1977 and 1986 (Allen & Santrock, 1993), indicating some improvement in the accessibility of advanced graduate degrees for African American women and increased motivation to achieve those degrees.

Many Asian American families have carried on from their original culture traditional gender roles associated with males and females. Asian females are often expected to bear the brunt of domestic duties, to raise children, and to be a "good" daughter-in-law. Asian American males are often raised to remain aloof, unemotional, and authoritative, especially concerning familial issues (Sue, 1989). There have been some studies, however, that suggest a loosening of these rigid, traditional gender roles for Asian American males and females. Although Asian American males may still appear as a figurative head of a family in public, in reality much decision-making power within the family in private is held by the Asian American female head of the household (Huang & Ying, 1989).

As with Asian American gender roles, the traditional role of the Mexican female was to provide for the children and take care of the home (Comas-Diaz, 1992). Likewise, the role for Mexican American males traditionally dictated a strong expectation of provider for the family. These differences are related to the concept of **machismo**. This concept involves many of the traditional expectations of the male gender role, such as being unemotional, strong, authoritative, aggressive, and masculine (see Table 5.1). However, recent research has shown that these gender differences for Mexican American males and females are also on the decrease. Mexican American women are increasingly sharing in decision making in the family, as well as taking on a more direct role in being a provider through work outside the home (Espin, 1993). Although adolescent Mexican American males are generally still given more freedom outside the home than are females, gender differences may be decreasing in the contemporary Mexican American family.

Gender role differentiation for Native Americans seems to depend heavily on the patriarchal or matriarchal nature of the tribal culture of origin. In patriarchal tribes, for example, women assume the primary responsibility for the welfare of the children and extended family members. But males of the Mescalero Apache tribe often take responsibility for children when they are with their families (Ryan, 1980). As with the other ethnic groups, the passage of time, increased interaction with people of other cultures and with mainstream American culture, and the movement toward urban areas seems to have influenced changes in these traditional values and expectations for Native American males and females.

Certainly, the picture I have painted for these ethnic groups is not universally true or salient for all males and females of these ethnic groups. Instead, they serve as generalized descriptions of the possible gender roles males and females of these ethnic groups have been socialized with in the past. There are many cultural and ethnic differences even within each of these four major groupings. As time passes and societal trends and cultural mores change, gender roles will also change both between and within each of these ethnic groups. As we are in a state of flux, it is important to remember that people of different ethnic and cultural backgrounds can and will have different gender role expectations despite appearances of overlap and similarity due to the fact that they all live in the same country and are influenced by the same mainstream culture.

The Influence of Culture on Gender

How can we understand the influence of culture on gender? Clearly, with the distinctions between definitions I have drawn here, a newborn has sex but no gender. Gender is a construct that develops in children as they are socialized in their environments. As children grow older, they learn specific behaviors and patterns of activities appropriate and inappropriate for their sex, and they either adopt or reject those gender roles.

Ensuring that reproduction occurs fulfills men's and women's **sex roles**. But what happens after that (and before that as well) is entirely dependent on a host of variables. One of these variables is culture. The biological fact and necessity of reproduction, along with other biological and physiological differences between men and women, leads to behavioral differences between men and women. In earlier days, these behavioral differences were no doubt reinforced by the fact that a division of labor was necessary—someone had to look after children while someone else had to find food for the family. No one person could have done it all. Thus, the existence of reproductive differences led to a division of labor advantageous to the family as a unit. These differences, in turn, produced differences in a variety of psychological traits and characteristics, including aggressiveness, nurturance, achievement, and so forth. Berry and his colleagues (1992) have suggested that the model presented in Figure 5.1 describes how cultural practices can affect gender differences in psychological characteristics, and I think it is an excellent springboard for understanding the effects of culture on gender. From my perspective, however, the important thing to remember is that the factors involved in understanding culture and gender that are outlined in Figure 5.1 are not static or unidimensional. Indeed, the entire system is dynamic and interrelated and feeds back on and reinforces itself. As a result, this system is not a linear unit with influences going in a single direction; it acquires a life of its own. And the life of this system is reinforced by the glue we know of as culture.

Consequently, different cultures produce different outcomes in this system. One culture may foster considerable equality between the sexes and relatively few differences between the sexes on cultural practices and psychological characteristics. Another culture may foster considerable differences between the sexes, their cultural practices related to reproduction, and psychological characteristics associated with sex roles. Some cultures may foster differences between the sexes in one direction

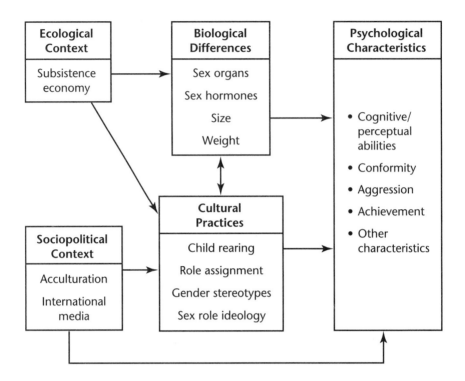

Figure 5.1 Framework for Examining Relationships among Contextual Variables and Gender Differences in Behavior

Source: Cross-Cultural Psychology: Research and Applications, by J. W. Berry, Y. H. Poortinga, M. H. Segall, and P. R. Dasen, p. 58. Copyright © 1992 Cambridge University Press. Reprinted with permission of Cambridge University Press.

(for example, males primary decision maker, females compliant and obedient); another culture may foster differences in the opposite direction.

The important point to remember is that different cultures arrive at varying outcomes even given the same process. Men and women will have gender-specific roles in any society or culture. In learning about gender across cultures, it is important to remember that all cultures encourage particular behavioral differences between the genders; that is, culture helps to define the roles, duties, and responsibilities appropriate for males and females.

Conclusion

Sex refers to the biological and physiological differences between males and females. Sex roles refer to behaviors expected of males and females in relation to their biological differences and reproduction. Gender, however, refers to the psychological and behavioral traits and characteristics cultures carve out using sex differences as a base. Gender roles refer to the degree to which a person adopts the gender-specific and appropriate behaviors ascribed by his or her culture.

Gender roles are different for males and females in all cultures. Some stereotypic notions about gender differences seem to be universal across cultures, such as aggressiveness, strength, and lack of emotionality for males, and weakness, submissiveness, and emotionality for females. Other research, however, has shown that the degree, and in some case the direction, of these differences varies across cultures. That is, not every culture will necessarily harbor the same gender differences in the same way as other cultures.

Examining gender differences in the United States is especially challenging because of the cultural and ethnic diversity within this single country and the influence of interactions with mainstream American culture. Although each ethnic group has its own cultural preferences for gender differentiation, some blending of the old with the new, the traditional with the modern appears to be taking place. Without evidence to the contrary, it is probably best to consider the blending as the addition of different cultural repertoires concerning gender differences rather than a subtraction from the old ways.

Recognizing that cultures differ in the degree to which they foster or discourage differences between the sexes is important to gaining a better grasp of the principles of psychology that underlie gender differences. At the same time, this knowledge allows us to critically examine both differences and similarities when they occur. These improvements and recognition have important ramifications to our practical lives as well.

As we meet people from different cultural backgrounds, we may encounter gender roles that are different from our own. Often, we feel strongly and negatively about them. Although our own feelings are indicative of our own personal outlook on those differences, we must exercise considerable care and caution in imposing our preferences on others. In most cases, people of other cultures feel just as strongly about their own way of living. Still, this is a delicate balancing act for all of us, because there is a fine line between cultural relativity and a social justification for oppression. Whereas the former is a desired state of comprehension, the latter is entirely unacceptable.

Glossary

gender The behaviors or patterns of activities a society or culture deems appropriate for men and women. These behavioral patterns may or may not be related to sex and sex roles, although they often are.

gender role   The degree to which a person adopts the gender-specific and appropriate behaviors ascribed by his or her culture.

gender role ideology   Judgments about what gender roles in a particular culture should or ought to be.

gender stereotype   The psychological or behavioral characteristics associated typically with men and women.

machismo   A concept related to Mexican American gender role differentiation that is characterized by many of the traditional expectations of the male gender role, such as being unemotional, strong, authoritative, aggressive, and masculine.

sex   The biological and physiological differences between men and women. The most obvious difference involves the anatomical differences of the reproductive systems for men and women.

sex roles   The behaviors and patterns of activities men and women may engage in that are directly related to their biological differences and the process of reproduction.

Suggested Readings

Berry, J. W., Poortinga, Y. H., Segall, M., & Dasen, P. R. (1992). *Cross-cultural psychology: Research and applications*. Cambridge: Cambridge University Press.

Williams, J., & Best, D. (1982). *Measuring sex stereotypes: A thirty-nation study*. Newbury Park, CA: Sage.

6

Culture and Work

We all spend an inordinate amount of time in our lives at work. Work and career are among the most important aspects of our lives. We often identify ourselves with our work and careers, and we arrange much of our personal lives—our homes, our families, and our hobbies and interests—around the interests of work and career.

For this reason, it is no wonder that the arena of work is of interest to psychologists. Many topics fall within the purview of study in this area, including leadership, motivation, productivity, job satisfaction, gender differences, and the like. In addition, the study of organizations is also germane to this area of psychology, including hiring, retention, and termination decisions and structures; hierarchies; communication; decision-making procedures; overall structure; and the like.

Because of the importance of work and career in our lives, it is important to glean the principles generated from psychological research and theorizing on these topics to improve our lives. As we do, however, we need to realize that the psychological and behavioral processes that occur at work, and that serve as the bases for these studies and principles, themselves occur in multifaceted contexts and milieus. One of these important contexts within which organizations and people exist, and within which work occurs, is culture. And, as we have been discussing throughout this book, it is important for us to examine the ways in which culture influences the psychological principles generated from research and the ways in which these principles may be similar, or different, across cultures.

This chapter will examine three of the many areas of work that may be influenced by culture: the meaning of work, work-related values, and international and intercultural business and work. These topics exemplify the considerable research that has been done on the topic of culture and organizations/work and should give you an idea of how work may be viewed and engaged in differently across people and cultures.

Cultural Similarities and Differences in the Meaning of Work

The first issue to consider is the possibility that the meaning of work differs across cultures. People construe themselves and their existence in relation to work differently across cultures, and these differences are related to meaningful dimensions of cultural variability. For example, people who are members of collectivistic cultures tend to have interdependent construals of their selves. That is, they tend to identify people around them, and their work organization itself, as fundamentally interrelated with themselves and as integral parts of their self-identities. This tendency is diminished in individualistic cultures, which tend to foster a view of self as independent, unique, and autonomous from others.

People of collectivistic cultures view their work groups and the work organizations (companies) to which they belong as a fundamental part of themselves. The bonds between these people and their work colleagues, and between themselves and their company, are stronger and fundamentally and qualitatively different from those for people with independent senses of self. Work, work colleagues, and the company become synonymous with the self.

People in individualistic cultures, however, have an easier time separating themselves from their jobs. They find it easier to distinguish between "work time" and "personal time." They make greater distinctions between company-based expense accounts and personal expenses. They also make greater distinctions between social and work activities, with regard to both their work colleagues and their business associates (potential clients, customers, and so forth.).

Cultural differences in the meaning of work can be manifest in other aspects of work as well. For example, in American culture, it is easy to think of work as a means to the accumulation of money (pay or salary) to make a living. In other cultures, especially collectivistic ones, work may be seen more as the fulfillment of an obligation to a larger group. In this situation, you would expect to find less movement of an individual from one job to another because of the social obligations the individual has toward the work organization to which he or she belongs and to the people that organization comprises. In individualistic cultures, however, it is easier to consider leaving one job and going to another because it is easier to separate jobs from the self. A different job will just as easily accomplish the same goals. Many of these cultural differences exist because of differences in work-related values.

Cultural Differences in Work-Related Values

People of different cultural backgrounds bring with them different values related to their work. These values span topics such as individual orientation and attitudes about work itself, attitudes about the organization and company loyalty, the importance of personal relationships with other members of the company, and so forth. Cultural similarities and differences in value orientations related to work can be the source of overall growth and financial gain or of conflict, frustration, and organizational stumbling.

The best-known study of work-related values was conducted by Hofstede (1980, 1984) in the 1960s and 1970s. His study involved employees at International Business Machines (IBM), a multinational corporation with offices in many different countries. In his original study (1980), Hofstede reported data collected from workers in 40 different countries. In a later study (1984), he reported data from an additional 10 countries. Altogether, more than 116,000 questionnaires were distributed to workers in these various countries, spanning upward of 20 different languages. In addition, 7 different occupational levels were included in the study.

The questionnaire itself contained approximately 160 items, of which 63 were related to work values. The questions clustered around four major themes: satisfaction, perception, personal goals and beliefs, and demographics. Hofstede identified four major dimensions of work-related values and computed overall scores for each country on each of these four dimensions. This approach allowed him to order the countries according to the score they had on each dimension. This approach, using country or group scores as the units of analysis, is called an ecological approach. This approach is slightly different from those that use individuals as the unit of analysis and can be used to identify and characterize national tendencies along these dimensions. However, a one-to-one correspondence with those same tendencies does not necessarily exist on the individual level within a country.

Hofstede called the four dimensions in his study power distance (PD), uncertainty avoidance (UA), individualism-collectivism (IC), and masculinity (MA). IC was introduced in Chapter 4; indeed, Hofstede's study was a major impetus to viewing and understanding cultures using a dimensional approach. Each of these dimensions is related to concrete differences in attitudes, opinions, beliefs, and behaviors within work organizations and forms the basis for understanding certain societal norms that exist in each of the countries in Hofstede's studies.

Power Distance

In organizations, hierarchical relationships based on status and power differences are necessary. Indeed, differentiating people according to their roles, functions, and positions within a company is vital to the successful operations of that organization. Work organizations are no different in this respect from any other organizations. The various statuses afforded different individuals within a hierarchy in a company come with certain benefits, rights, privileges, and power not afforded others. The "chain of command" within a company identifies the players and their roles. Each company decides these issues based on their importance for its continued functioning in the marketplace.

Each culture and all people within cultures develop ways of dealing with power and status differences. Power distance (PD) refers to the degree to which different cultures encourage or maintain power and status differences between interactants. Cultures high on PD develop rules, mechanisms, and rituals that serve to maintain and strengthen the status relationships among their members. Cultures low on PD, however, minimize status differences. In Hofstede's original study (1980), the Philippines, Mexico, Venezuela, and India had the highest scores on this dimension, suggesting that people in these countries maintained strong status differences. Countries such as New Zealand, Denmark, Israel, and Austria had the lowest marks on PD, suggesting that they minimized status and power differentials. The United States had scores slightly lower than the middle, reflecting some degree of minimizing of power differences.

According to Hofstede, cultural differences on PD are related to individual differences in behaviors that have consequences for their work. Table 6.1 summarizes those characteristics Hofstede gleaned not only from his research but from that of others as well. For example, managers in organizations in high PD cultures are seen as making decisions autocratically and paternalistically. Managers in organizations in low PD cultures, however, are observed making decisions only after more extensive consultation with their subordinates.

The behaviors listed in Table 6.1 are related to societal norms, which in turn have important consequences for organizational structure. In general, cultures high on PD foster organizations with greater centralization of organization and process, taller organizational pyramids, larger proportions of supervisory personnel, larger wage differentials, lower qualifications for lower strata of employees, and greater valuation of white collar

Table 6.1   Summary of Connotations of Power Distance Index (PDI) Differences Found in Survey Research

Low PDI Countries	High PDI Countries
Parents put less value on children's obedience.	Parents put high value on children's obedience.
Students put high value on independence.	Students put high value on conformity.
Authoritarian attitudes in students are a matter of personality.	Students show authoritarian attitudes as a social norm.
Managers seen as making decisions after consulting with subordinates.	Managers seen as making decisions autocratically and paternalistically.
Close supervision negatively evaluated by subordinates.	Close supervision positively evaluated by subordinates.
Stronger perceived work ethic: strong disbelief that people dislike work.	Weaker perceived work ethic: more frequent belief that people dislike work.
Managers more satisfied with participative superior.	Managers more satisfied with directive or persuasive superior.
Subordinates' preference for manager's decision-making style clearly centered on consultative, give-and-take style.	Subordinates' preference for manager's decision-making style polarized between autocratic-paternalistic and majority rule.
Managers like seeing themselves as practical and systematic; they admit a need for support.	Managers like seeing themselves as benevolent decision makers.
Employees less afraid of disagreeing with their boss.	Employees fear to disagree with their boss.
Employees show more cooperativeness.	Employees reluctant to trust each other.
Managers seen as showing more consideration.	Managers seen as showing less consideration.
Students have positive associations with "power" and "wealth."	Students have negative associations with "power" and "wealth."
Mixed feeling about employees' participation in management.	Ideological support for employees' participation in management.
Mixed feelings among managers about the distribution of capacity for leadership and initiative.	Ideological support among managers for a wide distribution of capacity for leadership and initiative.
Informal employee consultation possible without formal participation.	Formal employee participation possible without informal consultation.
Higher-educated employees hold much less authoritarian values than lower-educated ones.	Higher- and lower-educated employees show similar values about authority.

Source: G. Hofstede, *Culture's Consequences: International Differences in Work-Related Values,* p. 92. Copyright © 1980 Sage Publications. Reprinted by permission of Sage Publications, Inc.

as opposed to blue collar jobs. All these characteristics of work organizations and the nature of interpersonal relationships within companies can be considered as a natural consequence of social and cultural differences on power distance.

Uncertainty Avoidance

Uncertainty is a fact of life. No one can predict with 100% accuracy what the future holds for any of us. Although this is true for all of us as individuals, it is especially true for companies. Today's profits can easily turn into tomorrow's losses, and vice versa. How a market will react to a new product, revisions in old products, corporate restructuring, mergers and acquisitions, and all the other changes that occur within organizations and in the business world is a major source of uncertainty. With this uncertainty can come confusion, stress, and anxiety.

Every society and every organization develops its own ways to deal with the anxiety and stress associated with the uncertainty of the future. Often, these involve development of rituals, informal or written, concerning a code of conduct among employees, as seen in intracompany policies regarding communication or interpersonal relationships. These rules may also govern behavior between companies within a society, or across cultures, as witnessed in domestic and international laws governing business and interbusiness relationships.

Uncertainty avoidance (UA) is a dimension observed in Hofstede's (1980) study that described the degree to which different societies and different cultures develop ways to deal with the anxiety and stress of uncertainty. Cultures high on UA develop highly refined rules and rituals that are mandated and become part of the company rubric and normal way of operations. Companies in these cultures may be thought to be "rule oriented." In Hofstede's survey, Greece, Portugal, Belgium, and Japan were the four countries with the highest scores on this dimension. Cultures low on UA are less concerned with rules and rituals, have a more relaxed attitude concerning uncertainty and ambiguity, and have comparably fewer rules and rituals mandated for their employees. In Hofstede's study, Sweden, Denmark, and Singapore had the lowest scores on UA.

Cultural differences on UA are directly related to concrete differences in jobs and work-related behaviors. Table 6.2 lists the characteristics of people associated with cultures high or low on UA. For example, cultures high on UA tend to be associated with greater job stress than cultures low on UA. This is ironic, given that cultures high on UA are supposed to place greater emphasis on developing ways of dealing with the stress and anxiety produced by uncertainty. Perhaps the ways that are developed are so complex that they produce increased stress in the workers who have to abide by those rules and rituals!

Table 6.2 A Summary of Connotations of Uncertainty Avoidance Index (UAI) Differences Found in Survey Research

Low UAI Countries	High UAI Countries
Lower anxiety level in population.	Higher anxiety level in population.
Greater readiness to live by the day.	More worry about the future.
Lower job stress.	Higher job stress.
Less emotional resistance to change.	More emotional resistance to change.
Less hesitation to change employers.	Tendency to stay with the same employer.
Loyalty to employer is not seen as a virtue.	Loyalty to employer is seen as a virtue.
Preference for smaller organizations as employers.	Preference for larger organizations as employers.
Smaller generation gap.	Greater generation gap.
Lower average age in higher level jobs.	Higher average age in higher level jobs: gerontocracy.
Managers should be selected on other criteria than seniority.	Managers should be selected on the basis of seniority.
Stronger achievement motivation.	Less achievement motivation.
Hope of success.	Fear of failure.
More risk-taking.	Less risk-taking.
Stronger ambition for individual advancement.	Lower ambition for individual advancement.
Prefers manager career over specialist career.	Prefers specialist career over manager career.
A manager need not be an expert in the field he manages.	A manager must be an expert in the field he manages.
Hierarchical structures of organizations can be by-passed for pragmatic reasons.	Hierarchical structures of organizations should be clear and respected.
Preference for broad guidelines.*	Preference for clear requirements and instructions.
Rules may be broken for pragmatic reasons.	Company rules should not be broken.
Conflict in organizations is natural.*	Conflict in organizations is undesirable.
Competition between employees can be fair and right.	Competition between employees is emotionally disapproved of.
More sympathy for individual and authoritative decisions.	Ideological appeal of consensus and of consultative leadership.
Delegation to subordinates can be complete.*	However, initiative of subordinates should be kept under control.
Higher tolerance for ambiguity in perceiving others (higher LPC).	Lower tolerance for ambiguity in perceiving others (lower LPC).

*Based on studies by Laurent (1978).

(continued on next page)

Table 6.2 (continued)

Low UAI Countries	High UAI Countries
More prepared to compromise with opponents.	Lower readiness to compromise with opponents.
Acceptance of foreigners as managers.	Suspicion toward foreigners as managers.
Larger numbers prepared to live abroad.	Fewer people prepared to live abroad.
Higher tolerance for ambiguity in looking at own job (lower satisfaction scores).	Lower tolerance for ambiguity in looking at own job (higher satisfaction scores).
Citizen optimism about ability to control politicians' decisions.	Citizen pessimism about ability to control politicians' decisions.
Employee optimism about the motives behind company activities.	Employee pessimism about the motives behind company activities.
Optimism about people's amount of initiative, ambition, and leadership skills.	Pessimism about people's amount of initiative, ambition, and leadership skills.

Source: G. Hofstede, *Culture's Consequences: International Differences in Work-Related Values,* pp. 132–133. Copyright © 1980 Sage Publications. Reprinted by permission of Sage Publications, Inc.

Cultural differences on UA have concrete consequences for organizations and organizational structure. As described above, organizations located in cultures high on UA generally have more structured activities, more written rules, a greater number of specialists, more managers involved in details, more task-oriented managers, and more conformity in managerial style than do organizations in cultures low on UA. Organizations in high UA cultures also tend to have lower labor turnover, less ambitious employees, fewer risk-taking behaviors and ventures, and more ritualistic behavior.

Individualism-Collectivism

Individualism-collectivism (IC) is a dimension that has been used quite extensively to explain, understand, and predict cultural differences in a variety of contexts. IC refers to the degree to which a culture will foster individualistic tendencies as opposed to group or collectivistic tendencies. Individualistic cultures tend to foster development of autonomous, unique, and separate individuals. In these cultures, the needs, wishes, desires, and goals of individuals take precedence over group or collectivistic goals. Collectivistic cultures foster interdependence of individuals within groups. In these cultures, individuals sacrifice their own personal needs and goals for the sake of a common good.

Collectivistic cultural values foster more compliance with company policies and more conformity in group, section, or unit behavior. Collectivism also fosters a greater degree of reliance on group work and group orientation to company and organizational tasks. Harmony within groups, sections, or business units is valued more in collectivistic cultures, and members are more likely to engage in behaviors that ensure harmony and refrain from behaviors that threaten harmony. In Hofstede's study, subjects in the United States, Australia, Great Britain, and Canada were the most individualistic of all workers in the study. Peru, Pakistan, Columbia, and Venezuela were the most collectivistic.

IC differences between countries and cultures are associated with concrete differences in worker attitudes, values, beliefs, and behaviors about work and their companies. Table 6.3 summarizes the differences Hofstede gleaned from his and others' studies. For example, people in individualistic cultures tend to regard their personal time as important and make clear distinctions about their time and company time. People in individualistic cultures place more importance on freedom and challenge in their jobs, and initiative is generally encouraged on the job. These tendencies are generally not found in collectivistic cultures. In fact, such issues as freedom, independence, and initiative are normally frowned upon in collectivistic cultures.

IC cultural differences across countries and societies produce clear consequences for organizational structure and work in general (Hofstede, 1980). For example, organizations in individualistic cultures are not expected to look after their employees across their life span. Organizations in collectivistic cultures, however, are expected to do so, as they are morally responsible for the welfare of their employees for most of their lives. As a result, employees in individualistic cultures tend to have a more calculating or analytic view of their relationship to their companies, whereas employees of collectivistic cultures tend to view their relationship with their companies as moral in nature. Likewise, in individualistic cultures, employees are expected to defend their own personal interests; employees in collectivistic cultures can expect their companies to have their best interests at heart.

On the level of organizational policy, companies in individualistic cultures generally have policies, rules, and guidelines that will allow and encourage individual initiative and freedom; collectivistic cultures do not. Promotion and organizational advancement in individualistic cultures are generally based on accomplishment or achievement; in collectivistic cultures, promotions are generally based on seniority regardless of accomplishment.

Masculinity

Biological differences between men and women are a given. The question that every society, culture, and individual has to deal with is the degree to which the biological differences translate to practical differences in social

Table 6.3 Summary of Connotations of Individualism Index Differences Found in Survey and Related Research

Low IDV Countries	High IDV Countries
Importance of provisions by company (training, physical conditions).	Importance of employees' personal life (time).
Emotional dependence on company.	Emotional independence from company.
Large company attractive.	Small company attractive.
Moral involvement with company.	Calculative involvement with company.
Moral importance attached to training and use of skills in jobs.	More importance attached to freedom and challenge in jobs.
Students consider it less socially acceptable to claim pursuing their own ends without minding others.	Students consider it socially acceptable to claim pursuing their own ends without minding others.
Managers aspire to conformity and orderliness.	Managers aspire to leadership and variety.
Managers rate having security in their position more important.	Managers rate having autonomy more important.
Managers endorse "traditional" points of view, not supporting employee initiative and group activity.	Managers endorse "modern" points of view on stimulating employee initiative and group activity.
Group decisions are considered better than individual decisions.	However, individual decisions are considered better than group decisions.
Duty in life appeals to students.	Enjoyment in life appeals to students.
Managers choose duty, expertness, and prestige as life goals.	Managers choose pleasure, affections, and security as life goals.
Individual initiative is socially frowned upon: fatalism.	Individual initiative is socially encouraged.
More acquiescence in responses to "importance" questions.	Less acquiescence in responses to "importance" questions.
People thought of in terms of ingroups and outgroups; particularism.	People thought of in general terms; universalism.
Social relations predetermined in terms of ingroups.	Need to make specific friendships.
More years of schooling needed to do a given job.	Fewer years of schooling needed to do a given job.
More traffic accidents per 1000 vehicles.	Fewer traffic accidents per 1000 vehicles.
More traditional time use pattern.	More modern time use pattern.

roles, functions, or positions. Traditionally, these differences have existed, at least in the United States, with men generally being more assertive, dominant, and the primary wage earner. Women have traditionally been perceived as more nurturing, caring, and primarily concerned with family and child care issues (see also Chapter 5). This picture has been changing rapidly in the United States and continues to be a source of conflict, controversy, and confusion. Values concerning equity and equality have been infused in the workplace, and many American companies are still in transition to provide gender equity in the workplace.

The fourth dimension in Hofstede's study was labeled masculinity (MA). This label, however, implies gender differences and is somewhat misleading because almost all the employees who completed the questionnaire were male. Many of the items identified with this dimension, in fact, had more to do with materialism than relationships, and Hofstede interpreted this factor as identifying masculinity. Still, this dimension can be conceptually useful in understanding gender differences in the workplace. According to Hofstede, this dimension referred to the degree to which cultures would foster or maintain differences between the sexes in work-related values. Cultures high on MA—such as Japan, Austria, Venezuela, and Italy—were found to be associated with the greatest degree of sex differences in work-related values. Cultures low on MA—such as Denmark, Netherlands, Norway, and Sweden—had the fewest differences between the sexes.

Cultural differences on MA were associated with very concrete differences between the workers and the organizations. Table 6.4 summarizes these differences. For example, managers in cultures high on MA valued leadership, independence, and self-realization; cultures low on MA placed less importance on these constructs. Employees in high-MA cultures regarded earnings, recognition, advancement, and challenge as relatively more important than did employees in low-MA cultures. And fewer women were in mixed-sex jobs in organizations in high-MA cultures than in low-MA cultures.

There are interesting consequences for both organizational structure and employee relationships in the company as a result of cultural differences on MA (Hofstede, 1980). For example, young men in high-MA cultures generally expect to make a career in their jobs, and those who don't do so see themselves as failures. In high-MA cultures, organizational interests, needs, and goals are viewed as legitimate reasons to interfere in the personal and private lives of employees. There are generally fewer women in more qualified and better paid jobs in high-MA cultures, and those women who are in more qualified jobs are generally very assertive. There is generally more job stress in organizations located in high-MA cultures.

Table 6.4   Summary of Connotations of Masculinity Index Differences Found in Survey and Related Research

Low MAS Countries	High MAS Countries
Relationship with manager, cooperation, friendly atmosphere, living in a desirable area, and employment security relatively more important to HERMES employees.	Earnings, recognition, advancement, and challenge relatively more important to HERMES employees.
Managers relatively less interested in leadership, independence, and self-realization.	Managers have leadership, independence, and self-realization ideal.
Belief in group decisions.	Belief in the independent decision maker.
Students less interested in recognition.	Students aspire to recognition (admiration for the strong).
Weaker achievement motivation.	Stronger achievement motivation.
Achievement defined in terms of human contacts and living environment.	Achievement defined in terms of recognition and wealth.
Work less central in people's lives.	Greater work centrality.
People prefer shorter working hours to more salary.	People prefer more salary to shorter working hours.
Company's interference in private life rejected.	Company's interference in private life accepted.
Greater social role attributed to other institutions than corporation.	Greater social role attributed to corporation.
HERMES employees like small companies.	HERMES employees like large corporations.
Entire population more attracted to smaller organizations.	Entire population more attracted to larger organization.
Lower job stress.	Higher job stress.
Less skepticism as to factors leading to getting ahead.	Skepticism as to factors leading to getting ahead.
Students more benevolent (sympathy for the weak).	Students less benevolent.
Managers have more a service ideal.	Managers relatively less attracted by service role.
"Theory X" strongly rejected.	"Theory X" (employees dislike work) gets some support.
In HERMES, more women in jobs with mixed sex composition.	In HERMES, fewer women in jobs with mixed sex composition.
Smaller or no value differences between men and women in the same jobs.	Greater value differences between men and women in the same jobs.
Sex role equality in children's books.	More sex role differentiation in children's books.

Source: G. Hofstede, *Culture's Consequences: International Differences in Work-Related Values,* pp. 200–201. Copyright © 1980 Sage Publications. Reprinted by permission of Sage Publications, Inc.

Other Dimensions of Work-Related Values

Other studies of international and cross-cultural differences in work-related values have pointed to yet another important dimension of cultural difference. Working in collaboration with Hofstede, Michael Bond and his colleagues (Chinese Culture Connection, 1987; Hofstede & Bond, 1988) studied the work-related values and psychological characteristics of workers and organizations in Asian countries. No doubt much of the impetus for this line of research has been the surge of industry and business success of many Asian nations such as Japan, Hong Kong, and Korea. These researchers have identified another important dimension of work-related values, **Confucian dynamism**. Many of the principles and values found to be important to Asian companies are thought to be rooted in Confucian thought and principle. For example, some key principles of Confucian thought are:

- Unequal status relationships lead to a stable society.

- The family is typical of all social organizations.

- Virtue in life consists of working hard, acquiring useful skills and as much education as possible, not being a spendthrift, and persevering when faced with difficult tasks. (Brislin, 1993)

These principles translate to abstract values that play an important role not only in interpersonal relationships in business but also as organizational goals and principles. These include values for persistence and perseverance, ordering relationships by status and preserving this order, having a sense of thrift, and having a sense of shame. Also important are values that enforce personal steadiness and stability; protecting face and outward stance; respect for tradition, custom, history, and heritage; and reciprocating favors, greetings, and gifts.

Intercultural Conflicts in Business and Work

Cultural differences in the meaning of work and in work-related values provide the potential for considerable dynamism within organizations. Unfortunately, this organizational dynamism is often translated into conflict and controversy between people and organizations. In this final section, I explore the nature of some conflicts and controversies that arise because of differences in culture.

Intercultural Issues within and among Multinational Corporations

International business for **multinational corporations** is not just international; it is inter*cultural*. As has been discussed throughout this chapter, business organizations and work companies are affected in many different ways by the cultures in which they reside. Organizational structures are different in different cultures; organizational decision-making procedures are different in different cultures; people are different in different cultures, with differences in definitions and views of work itself, of work-related values, of identification between self and company, and in rules of interacting with other workers. In today's business world, succeeding in international business requires that businesses, and the people within them, gain intercultural competence as well as business competence. In particular, there are three different situations in which intercultural differences manifest themselves in the business situation: international negotiation, overseas assignments, and receiving workers from other countries.

International negotiation. The dual influences of improving communications technologies and changes in trade and tariff laws among countries has resulted in an increasing interdependence among countries for economic and business survival. This means that today more than ever before there are considerable burdens placed on multinational corporations that do business in many different countries. Extra burdens are also placed on domestic companies that need to negotiate with companies in other countries to obtain resources, sell products, and conduct other business activities.

In the arena of international negotiation, negotiators come not only as representatives of their companies but of their cultures as well. They bring with them all the issues of culture—customs, rituals, rules, and heritage—as they come to the negotiating table. Things that we are not even aware of play a role in these negotiation sessions, such as the amount of space between the people, how to greet each other, what to call each other, and what kinds of expectations we have of each other. The "diplomatic dance" that has been observed between American and Arab negotiators because of differences in personal space is but one example. People from Arab cultures tend to interact with others at a much closer distance than Americans are accustomed to. As the distance shrinks, Americans unconsciously edge backward, with the Arabs unconsciously edging forward, until they are almost chasing each other around the room.

Even little cultural differences can have big effects on international business. In the Japanese language, for example, the word for *yes* (*hai*) is also used as a conversational regulator, signaling to another person that you are listening to what they are saying (but not necessarily agreeing).

American negotiators have often heard this word being used as a regulator but interpreted it to mean yes. As you can imagine, considerable conflicts can arise, and have arisen, when a totally contradictory statement or refusal is given by the Japanese when they were using this word throughout the conversation. To the Japanese, they were merely saying "um hmm," while the Americans were interpreting this to be saying "yes." Such contradictions can lead to conflict, mistrust, the breakdown of negotiations, and the loss of business and good faith relations (see Okamoto, 1993).

One interesting arena in which cultural differences in negotiation occur is in entertainment. American businesspeople are used to "sitting down at the table and hammering out a deal." Japanese businesspeople may want to have dinner, have drinks, and play golf. The Japanese are more willing to engage in these activities because they are interested in developing a relationship with their business partners as people; it also gives them a good opportunity to make a judgment as to the character or integrity of potential partners, which is an important aspect of their business decisions. American businesspeople are primarily concerned with "the deal" and what is right for the company's bottom line. Many American business negotiators not used to the Japanese style of negotiating have become impatient with these activities, as it seems that they never get to talk business. Many Japanese negotiators have been put on the spot by American negotiators, feeling like they have been thrust into a situation and forced to make a decision they cannot possibly make. Needless to say, these cultural differences in negotiation styles have led to many a breakdown in international business negotiations.

Overseas assignments. Many multinational corporations with subsidiaries and business partners in other countries are finding it increasingly necessary to send workers abroad for extended periods of time. In many cases, worker exchange and overseas assignments are the result of the need to train employees and business units in another country in skills that are resident only there. When someone is sent abroad on an overseas assignment, myriad potential problems arise. Of course, problems occur at work because of all the cultural differences discussed in this chapter. But an added problem is limited language skills on the part of both the person on assignment and his or her hosts. Differences in expectations of the person on assignment and his or her hosts can be a major stumbling block to efficiency and progress.

In the United States, we would not hesitate in today's world to send a woman on assignment, either in negotiation or long term. In some other cultures, however, a woman would not be taken as seriously as a man. This will play out in very frustrating ways, such as not being looked at during a conversation or having questions directed to a man when the woman is the recognized leader or expert on an assignment team.

Ironically, many of the most pressing problems for people on overseas assignments occur not at work but in other aspects of living in a foreign country. There are often major differences in lifestyle, customs, and behaviors that overshadow cultural differences at work. If an individual goes on overseas assignment with his or her family, there is the added problem of their adjustment to the new culture, especially if children are involved and they need to be in school.

Despite the potential problems, there are also a number of advantages. People who go on overseas assignments have a tremendous opportunity to learn new skills and new ways of doing their work that can help them when they return. They may learn a new language and customs, which will broaden their perspectives. They may make new friends and business acquaintances, and this type of networking may have business as well as personal payoffs in the future. Foreign assignment is an important activity in today's international business world that promises to play an even larger role in the global village of the future. Completing these assignments to the best of our abilities requires us to understand all the influences of culture on these activities, both in and out of the workplace.

Receiving foreign workers. American companies are hosting more and more workers from other countries. Joint ventures between American and Asian and European countries have increased over the past 10 years. One result is an influx of workers from these other countries, and cultures, to the United States. Two good examples of this that have grabbed the nation's attention in the past are the joint ventures between American and Japanese and American and German automobile manufacturers.

Many of the problems that arise when we send workers overseas also are apparent when we receive foreign workers. Often, managers from another culture will come to supervise production or assembly. They bring with them all the expectations, customs, and rituals they learned and that were developed in their home country. Often, they find that those ways of business do not work in the United States because the people are different and the system is different. Families of workers who come to the United States also face many of the same problems as the families of U.S. workers overseas. One response by many Japanese companies in the Los Angeles area has been to establish little Japanese villages and apartments where the lifestyle and customs can be preserved to make the transition easier. Of course, these are not without controversy. They serve to maintain barriers between people just as much as they are a solution for some problems.

Nevertheless, despite the potential problems associated with receiving foreign workers, many of the advantages that exist for overseas assignments exist for receiving people from abroad as well. The ability to reap these benefits, of course, depends on the openness of the host company and organization to learn and the goodwill and intent of the employee and the company to engage in a mutually beneficial partnership.

Issues of Cultural Diversity in Domestic Work Organizations

One of the hottest issues in corporate America today concerns diversity. No doubt this is such a crucial issue in the United States because of the diverse nature of the American population and workforce. The United States is home to people of many different races and ethnicities and cultures. Within this "mixed salad" of cultures are generational differences; some workers are first-generation immigrants, and others come from many generations in the United States.

Many of the issues raised in dealing with people across countries and cultures are relevant for domestic work organizations as well. People come to work with different expectations, and these differences can lead to intercultural clashes. Cultural differences in the management of time and people, in identification with work, and in making decisions all are potential areas of conflict. People in the United States come to work with differences in work-related values and in the degree to which they respect or minimize power and status differences between them. People also come to work with differences in how they regard the sexes and how to manage uncertainty.

The challenge facing most American companies today with regard to cultural diversity is the wide range of people and cultures that can exist within any single work organization or business section. The problems that can occur when two cultures clash can be magnified many times over when people from multiple cultures are thrust together to interact with one another to achieve a common goal. Indeed, this is a very difficult problem because, at its base, people from different cultural backgrounds differ on their perceptions of goals and on means to achieve those goals.

What solutions exist? Many successful companies have met this challenge by making explicit what kinds of communication styles, decision making, productivity, and worker behaviors are important for the success of the company. Above and beyond that, they have created temporary **organizational cultures** in which their employees can move and adapt without fear of losing themselves or their own personal cultures. Many companies have designed ways not only of avoiding problems but also of handling problems effectively and constructively when they do occur, having the realistic vision that such problems are inevitable when different people come together. Although negotiating all this requires additional work and effort by companies and people just when resources seem to be getting scarcer and scarcer, organizations that have managed to do so generally realize greater benefits to the bottom line.

Conclusion

The world of work is an important part of all of our lives. As adults, we spend a major portion of our lives at work. Work takes on many different meanings for all of us. Despite differences in those meanings, few can doubt that we spend much time, effort, and energy in our lives at work and in business organizations. As time goes on, issues of culture and cultural differences with regard to work and organizations will become even larger and more important than they are today. The world is shrinking before our eyes, as improvements in communication and travel technology bring previously distant lands closer to us than ever before. The growing interdependence among countries, and the businesses and industries of those countries, promises to bring companies increasingly together. And along with those companies and countries come people with different cultural backgrounds.

In the final analysis, business is people. Products, goods, services, and warranties are important, but business leaders in international as well as domestic companies, large and small alike, agree that the most important ingredient to successful business is people. Our "people" skills are our most important business asset. Our ability to manage, guide, and lead others is a reflection of people skills. Our ability to search for prospective customers, to develop relationships, to negotiate contracts, to close sales, and to follow up are all dependent on people skills. Our ability to interact with bosses, presidents, and chairpersons of the board is dependent on people skills. Excellent products, goods, and services make our jobs easier, but in the final analysis, *good business is good people.*

Yet the differences that people bring with them to the job, both internationally and domestically, present challenges unprecedented in the modern industrialized period of history. These challenges, of differences among people due to differences in culture, are being met by business, government, and private organizations in the form of more research and education about cultural diversity as it relates to work. As we move toward a greater appreciation of cultural similarities and differences, particularly those that contribute to the diversity we observe in the workplace, we will gain a better appreciation for the approaches to work, management, and leadership that have been successful in different cultures. As we confront the challenges of diversity in the future, we need to move away from a perspective of managing a nuisance variable to viewing it as a potential resource for tapping into products, services, and activities that will make companies more efficient, productive, and profit-able. By tapping into diversity rather than managing it, perhaps we can increase international and intercultural cooperation in business and among people in general.

Glossary

Confucian dynamism A dimension of work-related values important to Asian companies and thought to be rooted in Confucian thought and prin-ciples.

multinational corporations Work organizations that have subsidiaries and satellite offices and work units in more than a single country.

organizational culture Aspects of an organization that serve as a macrolevel climate or atmosphere within which employees must operate. As a macrolevel variable, organizational culture has an impact on how people within an orga-nization think, feel, and behave.

Suggested Readings

Hofstede, G. (1980). *Culture's consequences: International differences in work-related values.* Newbury Park, CA: Sage.
Hofstede, G., & Bond, M. (1988). Confucius & economic growth: New trends in culture's consequences. *Organizational Dynamics, 16*(4), 4–21.
Lammers, C. J., & Hickson, D. J. (Eds). (1979). *Organizations alike and unlike: International and interinstitutional studies in the sociology of organizations.* London: Routledge & Kegan Paul.

Abnormal Psychology

One of the most active areas of cross-cultural inquiry is the examination of the role of culture in understanding, assessing, and treating abnormal behavior. Several major themes have guided research and thinking in abnormal psychology. First and foremost are questions concerning definitions of abnormality: What is abnormal behavior? A second set of questions relates to the expression of abnormal behavior and our ability to detect it (assessment). A third question concerns how we are able to treat abnormal behavior when it is detected.

These questions have special significance in relation to culture, as culture adds an important wrinkle in approaches to abnormality and treatment (Marsella, 1979). Do definitions of normality and abnormality vary across cultures, or are there universal standards of abnormality? Do cultures vary in rates of abnormal behavior? Is abnormal behavior expressed in the same way across cultures, or can we identify culturally distinct patterns of abnormal behavior?

The answers to these questions have gained importance in the past two decades as psychologists and other mental health professionals have questioned the cultural sensitivity of traditional methods of assessing and treating individuals with psychological disorders. Indeed, as this chapter will illustrate, the answers to these questions have important implications for how we understand, identify, and intervene to change abnormal behavior.

Defining Abnormality

Consider the following scenario:

A woman is in the midst of a group of people but seems totally unaware of her surroundings. She is talking loudly to no one in particular, often using

98

words and sounds the people around her find unintelligible. When questioned later about her behavior, she reports that she had been possessed by the spirit of an animal and was talking with a man who had recently died.

Some Traditional Viewpoints

Is this woman's behavior abnormal? In defining abnormal behavior, psychologists usually adopt one of several different approaches. These include a statistical approach and applications of criteria of impairment or inefficiency, deviance, and subjective distress.

From a **statistical-comparison approach**, the woman's behavior could be defined as abnormal because its occurrence is rare or infrequent. Being out of touch with one's surroundings, having delusions (mistaken beliefs) that one is an animal, and talking with the dead are not common experiences. One of the problems with this approach to defining abnormality, however, is that not all rare behavior is disordered, nor is all disordered behavior rare! Composing a concerto and speaking four languages are behaviors that are uncommon yet are generally viewed as highly desirable. Conversely, drinking to the point of drunkenness occurs quite often in the United States (and in many other countries), but repeated drunkenness is nevertheless widely recognized as a sign of a possible substance abuse disorder.

Another approach for defining abnormality focuses on whether an individual's behavior is associated with impairment or inefficiency in carrying out customary roles. It may be hard to imagine the woman described in the scenario carrying out normal daily functions—caring for herself and working—while she believes herself to be an animal. In many instances, psychological disorders do involve serious impairments or a reduction in an individual's overall functioning. This, however, is not always the case. Some people suffering from **bipolar disorder** (manic–depressives) report enhanced productivity during manic episodes.

If we examine the woman's behavior in terms of deviance, we might also conclude that it is abnormal because it seems to go against social norms. But not all behavior that is socially deviant can be considered abnormal or psychologically disordered. For example, many people continue to believe that homosexuality is deviant, although it is no longer classified as a mental disorder (American Psychiatric Association, 1987). Also, although some in this culture may view homosexuality as abnormal, in other cultures and at various periods in history homosexuality has been widely practiced and tolerated. Using societal norms as a criterion for abnormality is thus difficult not only because norms change over time, but because they are subjective. What one member of a society or culture considers deviant, another may accept.

Reliance on reports of **subjective distress** to define abnormal behavior is also problematic. Whether a person experiences distress as a consequence of abnormal behavior may depend on how others treat him or her. For example, if the woman in the scenario is ridiculed, shunned, and viewed as "sick" because of her behavior, she may well experience distress. Conversely, if she is seen as having special powers and is part of an accepting circle, she may not be distressed at all.

As can be seen, each of the more or less traditional viewpoints used by psychologists has advantages as well as disadvantages. These issues become even more complex when culture is considered. Definitions of abnormality may vary both within and across cultures.

Cross-Cultural Viewpoints of Abnormality

Dissatisfaction with traditional definitions of abnormality has led some cross-cultural investigators to argue that we can understand and identify abnormal behavior only if we take the cultural context into account. This viewpoint suggests that we must apply a principle of cultural relativism to abnormality. For example, the woman's behavior in the scenario might appear disordered if it occurred on a street corner in a large U.S. city. It could, however, appear appropriate and understandable if it occurs in the context of a shamanistic ceremony in which she is serving as healer. Cultures that hold beliefs in supernatural interventions are able to clearly distinguish when trance states and talking with spirits are an acceptable part of a healer's behavioral repertoire and when the same behaviors would be considered a sign of disorder (Murphy, 1976). Examples of such cultures include the Yoruba in Africa and an Eskimo tribe in Alaska.

Some behaviors, particularly those associated with **psychosis** (such as delusions and hallucinations), are universally recognized as abnormal (Murphy, 1976). However, some investigators (for example, Kleinman, 1988; Marsella, 1979, 1980) argue that abnormality and normality are culturally determined concepts. These investigators point to the fact that cultures differ in their beliefs about and attitudes toward abnormal behavior.

Reliance on reports of subjective distress to define abnormal behavior is also problematic when considering abnormality across cultures. There is some indication that cultural groups vary in the degree of distress they report experiencing in association with psychological disorders. For example, Kleinman (1988) describes research indicating that depressed Chinese and African individuals report less guilt and shame than do depressed Euro-American and European individuals. The Chinese and African individuals, however, do report more somatic complaints. These findings may reflect cultural variations in response set, discussed in Chapter 1. Some cultural groups may have values that prohibit reporting or focusing on subjective distress, in contrast to Western notions of the importance of self-disclosure.

Whether to accept universal or culturally relative definitions of abnormality is a source of continuing controversy in the field of cross-cultural psychology. This tension can be seen as well in considering the expression of abnormality across cultures.

Expression of Abnormality across Cultures

The focus of much of the cross-cultural study of abnormality has been on determining whether the rates and manifestations of psychological disorders vary across cultures. The two disorders studied most extensively are schizophrenia and depression, typically using diagnostic criteria and assessment procedures developed in Western psychology and psychiatry. This approach can be characterized as basically an "etic" approach that assumes universally accepted definitions of abnormality and methodology (review Chapter 1 for a definition of *emic* and *etic*).

In contrast to this etic approach to cross-cultural study of abnormality, there have also been some ethnographic reports of **culture-bound syndromes.** These are forms of abnormal behavior observed only in certain sociocultural milieus. Findings concerning different rates and courses of disorder across cultures, and of culturally distinct forms of disorder, suggest the importance of culture in shaping the expression of abnormal behavior.

Cultural Variations in Schizophrenia

Schizophrenia is part of a "group of psychotic disorders characterized by gross distortions of reality; withdrawal from social interaction; and disorganization of perception, thought, and emotion" (Carson, Butcher, & Coleman, 1988, p. 322). Some common theories concerning the etiology (causes) of schizophrenia give primacy to biological factors (for example, excess dopamine or some other biochemical imbalance). Others emphasize family dynamics (for example, expression of hostility to ill persons). The **diathesis-stress model of schizophrenia** suggests that individuals with a biological predisposition to the disorder (diathesis) may develop the disorder following exposure to environmental stressors.

Cross-cultural studies of schizophrenia have provided important information about the expression of this disorder across cultures. The World Health Organization (WHO, 1973, 1979, 1981), for example, sponsored the International Pilot Study of Schizophrenia (IPSS) to compare the prevalence and course of the disorder in several countries: Colombia, the former Czechoslovakia, Denmark, England, India, Nigeria, the former Soviet Union, Taiwan, and the United States. Following rigorous training in using the research assessment tool, psychiatrists in each of the countries achieved good reliability in diagnosing schizophrenia in patients included in the study. As a result, WHO investigators were able to identify a set of symptoms that were present across all cultures in the schizophrenic samples. These symptoms include lack of insight, auditory and verbal hallucinations, and ideas of reference (assuming one is the center of attention) (Leff, 1977).

The WHO studies are widely cited to bolster arguments for the universality of schizophrenia. But some important cross-cultural differences were found as well. In a finding that took the investigators by surprise, the course of the illness was shown to progress better for patients in developing countries compared to those in highly industrialized countries. Patients in Colombia, India, and Nigeria recovered at faster rates than those in England, the former Soviet Union, or the United States. These differences were attributed to cultural factors such as extended kin networks and the tendency to return to work in developing countries.

The researchers also noted differences in symptom expression across cultures. Patients in the United States were less likely to demonstrate lack of insight and auditory hallucinations than were Danish or Nigerian patients. These findings may be related to cultural differences in values associated with insight and self-awareness, which are highly regarded in the United States, but not as much so in the other countries. Also, there may have been cultural differences in the tolerance for these types of symptom profiles; the Nigerian culture as a whole is more accepting of the presence of voices. Nigerian and Danish patients, however, were more likely to demonstrate **catatonia** (extreme withdrawal or agitation).

Kleinman (1988) and Leff (1981) discussed some of the methodological problems that plagued the WHO studies. For instance, the assessment tool failed to tap culturally unique experiences and expressions of disorder. Kleinman also noted that the samples were made artificially homogeneous because of the selection criteria. He argued that the findings of cross-cultural differences might have been greater still had not the heterogeneity of the sample been reduced.

Other cross-cultural comparisons of rates and expression of schizophrenia (Leff, 1977; Murphy, 1982) have also found evidence of cultural variations. Murphy (1982) found that rates of admission for schizophrenia are four times higher in Ireland compared to England and Wales. These findings suggested that some features of Irish culture (sharp wit, ambivalence toward individuality) may have accounted for the cultural differences. In an early study of New York psychiatric cases, Opler and Singer (1959) found that Irish-American schizophrenic patients were more likely to experience paranoid delusions than were Italian-American schizophrenic patients. The authors cited cultural variations in parenting to account for the difference. A study of Japanese schizophrenics (Sue & Morishima, 1982) indicated that they are more likely than Euro-American counterparts to be withdrawn and passive, in conformity to cultural values.

Recent studies of schizophrenics have tested the theory that expressed emotion—family communication characterized by hostility and overinvolvement—increases the risk of relapse. The expressed-emotion construct is important because it suggests that family and social interactions influence the course of schizophrenia. These interactions are in turn influenced by cultural values. Research indicates that expressed emotion predicts relapse in Western samples (Mintz, Mintz, & Goldstein, 1987). Kleinman (1988), however, notes the difficulties in using this construct in other cultures, particularly in those that emphasize nonverbal communication. Karno and associates (1987) reported that expressed emotion also predicts relapse in Mexican Americans, but Kleinman (1988) questions whether measures of expressed emotion developed in one cultural context have validity in another.

Reports of cultural differences in diagnosis have also raised questions about the validity of assessment techniques used in cross-cultural comparisons of schizophrenia and other disorders (Kleinman, 1988; Leff, 1977). In a reanalysis of some of the early WHO data, Leff (1977) found that U.S. psychiatrists were more likely to give diagnoses of schizophrenia than were psychiatrists in England, and less likely to give diagnoses of depression. Abebimpe (1981) and others (Thomas & Sillen, 1972) have documented that African Americans are more likely than Euro-Americans to receive diagnoses of schizophrenia rather than depression, even when the symptom picture is the same. Racial bias seems to account for some of the differential pattern (Thomas & Sillen, 1972), and cultural differences in expression of symptomatology may also be important.

Cultural Variations in Depression

Depressive disorder involves the symptoms of "intense sadness, feelings of futility and worthlessness, and withdrawal from others" (Sue, Sue, & Sue, 1990, p. 325). Depression is often also characterized by physical changes (such as sleep and appetite disturbances) as well as emotional and behavioral changes (Berry, Poortinga, Segall, & Dasen, 1992). Like schizophrenia, depression is one of the most common psychological disorders in the United States. In a large-scale study, Myers et al. (1984) found that 3% of the adult male population and 7% of the adult female population had experienced a depressive disorder in the previous six-month period. Lifetime prevalence rates for depression are also high, sometimes as high as 26% for women and 12% for men (American Psychiatric Association, 1987, cited in Sue, Sue, & Sue, 1990). There is also some evidence to suggest that the incidence rate for depression has risen over the last few decades (Robins et al., 1984).

Cross-cultural studies of depression have widely documented variations in depressive symptomatology. Some cultural groups (such as the Nigerians) are less likely to report extreme feelings of worthlessness. Others (such as the Chinese) are more likely to report somatic complaints (Kleinman, 1988). As with schizophrenia, rates of depression also vary from culture to culture (Marsella, 1980). Leff (1977) argues that cultures vary in terms of their differentiation and communication of emotional terminology, and hence in how they experience and express depression.

In arguing for a culturally relative definition of depression, Kleinman (1988, p. 25) writes that

> depression experienced entirely as low back pain and depression experienced entirely as guilt-ridden existential despair are such substantially different forms of illness behavior with distinctive symptoms, patterns of help seeking, and treatment responses that although the disease in each instance may be the same, the illness, not the disease, becomes the determinative factor. And one might well ask, is the disease even the same?

Earlier, Kleinman (1978) argued that depressive disease reflects a biologically based disorder, whereas depressive illness refers to the personal and social experience of depression. Although Kleinman accepts the idea that depressive disease is universal, he argues that the expression and course of the illness are culturally determined.

Marsella (1979, 1980) also argues for a culturally relative view of depression. He states that depression takes a primarily affective form in cultures with strong objective orientations (that is, cultures that emphasize individualism). In these cultures, feelings of loneliness and isolation would dominate the symptom picture. Somatic symptoms such as headaches would be dominant in subjective cultures (those having a more communal structure). Marsella (1979) has also proposed that depressive symptom patterns will differ across cultures due to cultural variations in sources of stress as well as in resources for coping with the stress.

Culture-Bound Syndromes

Perhaps the strongest evidence for applying cultural relativism to abnormality comes from ethnographic reports of culture-bound syndromes. Using primarily emic (culture-specific) approaches involving ethnographic examination of behavior within a specific cultural context, anthropologists and psychiatrists have identified several apparently unique forms of psychological disorders. Some similarities between symptoms of these culture-specific disorders and those recognized across cultures have been observed. The particular patterning of culture-specific symptoms, however, typically does not fit the diagnostic criteria of psychological disorders recognized in Western classification schemes.

The most widely observed culture-bound syndrome has been identified in several countries in Asia (Malay, Philippines, Thailand). *Amok* is a disorder characterized by sudden rage and homicidal aggression. It is thought to be brought on by stress, sleep deprivation, and alcohol consumption (Carson, Butcher, & Coleman, 1988) and has been observed primarily in males. Several stages of the disorder have been identified, ranging from extreme withdrawal prior to the assaultive behavior to exhaustion and amnesia after the rage. The term "running amok" derives from observations of this disorder.

Witiko (also known as *windigo*) is a disorder that has been identified in Algonquin Indians in Canada. It involves the belief that one has been possessed by the witiko spirit—a man-eating monster. Cannibalistic behavior may result, along with suicidal ideation to avoid acting on the cannibalistic urges (Carson, Butcher, & Coleman, 1988).

Anorexia nervosa is a disorder that has been identified in the West but has not been observed in Third World countries (Swartz, 1985). The disorder is characterized by a distorted body image, fear of becoming fat, and a serious loss of weight associated with food restraining or purging. Several factors have been cited as possible causes of this disorder, including cultural emphasis on thinness as an ideal for women, constricted sex roles, and an individual's fears of being out of control or of taking on adult responsibilities.

Kiev (1972) and Yap (1974) reviewed the literature on these and other culture-bound syndromes, including *latah* (characterized by hysteria and echolalia, observed primarily in women in Malay); *koro* (impotence resulting from fear that the penis is retracting, observed in Southeast Asian men); and *susto* (characterized by depression and apathy thought to reflect "soul loss," observed in Indians of the Andean highlands). Yap (1974) has attempted to organize information concerning culture-bound syndromes into a classification scheme that parallels Western diagnostic schemes. Thus, latah and susto are viewed as unique cultural expressions of universal primary fear reactions. Amok is similarly viewed as a unique cultural expression of a universal rage reaction. Yap recognizes that his attempt to subsume culture-bound syndromes into a universal classification scheme may be premature, particularly because Western clinical tools and methods of research may make it difficult to assess culturally diverse expressions of abnormal behavior.

Pfeiffer (1982) has identified four dimensions for understanding culture-bound syndromes. He argues that culture-specific areas of stress may contribute to the syndromes. Such areas of stress include family and societal structure and ecological conditions. For example, koro might be best understood as resulting from the unique cultural emphasis on potency in certain cultures that emphasize paternal authority. Culture-specific shaping of conduct and interpretations of conduct may also account for the development of culture-bound syndromes. Pfeiffer suggests that cultures may implicitly approve patterns of exceptional behavior, as in the case of amok, in which aggression against others "broadly follows the patterns of societal expectations" (p. 206). Finally, Pfeiffer argues that how a culture interprets exceptional behavior will be linked to culture-specific interventions. For example, interventions to heal the soul loss associated with susto will involve sacrifices carried out by a native healer to appease the earth so that it will return the soul.

Pfeiffer (1982) and others (Kleinman, 1988; Marsella, 1979) argue that it is impossible to use current Western classification schemes to understand culture-bound syndromes because the latter are experienced from a qualitatively different point of view. They argue that culture shapes the experience of psychological disorder, both in determining the expression of symptoms of universal disorders and in contributing to the emergence of culture-specific disorders. Kleinman and Marsella go a step further, arguing that recognition of the role of culture in shaping abnormal behavior requires that we reexamine the way we assess and treat individuals with psychological disorders.

Assessment and Treatment of Abnormal Behavior across Cultures

Assessment of abnormal behavior involves identifying and describing an individual's symptoms "within the context of his or her overall level of functioning and environment" (Carson, Butcher, & Coleman, 1988, p. 531). The tools and methods of assessment should be sensitive to cultural and other environmental influences on behavior and functioning. The literature involving standard assessment techniques, however, indicates that there may be problems of bias or insensitivity when psychological tests and other methods developed in one cultural context are used to assess behavior in other cultures.

Tseng and McDermott (1981) write that the goal of treatment of abnormal behavior is to "relieve symptoms and help the patient become a healthier, more mature person . . . better able to deal with life and the problems it presents" (p. 264). They note that although there may be widespread agreement concerning the general goal of treatment, cultures will vary in their definitions of what is considered "healthy" or "mature." There also may be cultural differences in perceptions of problems and in preferred strategies for coping with problems (Terrell, 1992). As Berry et al. (1992) note, cultural beliefs and practices influence treatment because they shape both the therapist's and the client's definitions and understandings of the problem. As with assessment, however, traditional approaches to treatment of abnormal behavior may prove insensitive or inappropriate when applied across cultures.

Most psychology texts do a good job of describing traditional methods of assessment: various psychological tests, classification and diagnostic schemes, interview procedures, and observations. Similarly, different approaches to treatment of psychological disorders are amply covered, including psychoanalytic, behavioral, and humanistic approaches to therapy. In this section, we briefly review the literature on assessment and treatment across cultures, paying attention to models proposed to address cultural issues in assessment and treatment.

Issues in Cross-Cultural Assessment of Abnormal Behavior

We have seen how the definition and expression of abnormal behavior may vary within and across cultures. Traditional tools of clinical assessment, however, are primarily based on a standard definition of abnormality and use a standard set of classification criteria for evaluating problematic behavior. Therefore, the tools may have little meaning in cultures with varying definitions, however well translated they are into the native language, and they may mask or fail to capture culturally specific expressions of disorder (Marsella, 1979). The assessment problems encountered in studying schizophrenia and depression across cultures illustrate the limitations of traditional assessment methods.

Leff (1986) commented on the ethnocentric bias of such clinical interview procedures as the Present State Examination and the Cornell Medical Index. The Present State Examination was used to diagnose schizophrenia in the WHO studies described earlier. In a psychiatric survey of the Yoruba in Nigeria, investigators had to supplement the latter instrument to include culture-specific complaints such as feeling "an expanded head and goose flesh."

Standard diagnostic instruments to measure depressive disorder may also miss important cultural expressions of the disorder in Africans (Beiser, 1985) and Native Americans (Manson, Shore, & Bloom, 1985). In an extensive study of depression among Native Americans (Manson & Shore, 1981; Manson, Shore, & Bloom, 1985), the American Indian Depression Schedule (AIDS) was developed to assess and diagnose depressive illness. The investigators found that depression among Hopi Indians includes symptoms not measured by standard measures of depression such as the Diagnostic Interview Schedule (DIS) and the Schedule for Affective Disorders and Schizophrenia (SADS). These measures, based on diagnostic criteria found in the Diagnostic and Statistical Manual of Mental Disorders (APA, 1987), failed to capture the short, but acute dysphoric moods sometimes reported by the Hopi (Manson, Shore, & Bloom, 1985).

In reviewing the limitations of standard assessment techniques, several authors (Higginbotham, 1979; Marsella, 1979; Lonner & Ibrahim, 1989) have offered guidelines for developing measures to be used in cross-cultural assessment of abnormal behavior. They suggest that sensitive assessment methods examine sociocultural norms of healthy adjustment as well as culturally based definitions of abnormality. Higginbotham (1979) also suggests the importance of examining culturally sanctioned systems of healing and influence on abnormal behavior. There is evidence that people whose problems match cultural categories of abnormality are more likely to seek folk healers (Leff, 1986). Failure to examine indigenous healing systems would thus overlook some expressions of disorders. Assessment of culturally sanctioned systems of cure should also enhance the planning of treatment strategies, one of the major goals of traditional assessment (Carson, Butcher, & Coleman, 1988).

Issues in the Treatment of Abnormal Behavior across Cultures

In the past two decades, there has been a growing literature indicating that culturally diverse clients may be underserved or inappropriately served by traditional treatment methods. In a pioneering study of ethnic differences in response to standard mental health services in the Seattle area, Sue (1977) found lower rates of utilization of services among Asian Americans and Native Americans compared to Euro-Americans and African Americans. More dramatically, he found that all the groups except Euro-Americans had high dropout rates and relatively poorer treatment outcomes. A later study in the Los Angeles area showed similar findings (Sue, 1991). Sue (1977; Sue & Zane, 1987) concluded that low utilization and high attrition rates were due to the cultural insensitivity of standard treatment methods.

In efforts to fashion more culturally sensitive services, Sue and others (Comas-Diaz & Jacobsen, 1991; Higginbotham, 1979; Sue & Zane, 1987; Tseng & McDermott, 1981) suggest that treatment methods should be modified to improve their fit with the worldviews and experiences of culturally diverse clients. For example, psychoanalytic approaches are derived from a worldview assuming that unconscious conflicts (probably sexual) give rise to abnormal behavior. This worldview may reflect the experience of the well-to-do Austrian women whom Freud treated and based many of his theoretical assumptions on. A therapeutic approach based on such a worldview, however, may prove inappropriate in cultures that attribute abnormality either to natural factors (for example, physical problems or being out of harmony with one's environment) or supernatural causes (for example, spirit possession). Cultural systems of cure and healing may be effective precisely because they operate within a particular culture's worldview (Tseng & McDermott, 1981). Thus, a spiritual ceremony performed by native shaman (priest or healer) might prove to be a more effective treatment of the culture-bound syndrome of susto than would a cognitive-behavioral approach.

A long line of research on preferences for therapeutic approaches in ethnically different populations in the United States indicates that non–Euro-American clients tend to prefer action-oriented therapy rather than the nondirective approaches characteristic of psychoanalytic and humanistic therapy (Sue & Zane, 1987). There is also some indication that culturally diverse clients prefer to see therapists who are similar in terms of cultural background and gender. More recent research, however, indicates that similarity of worldviews and attitudes to treatment between client and therapist may be more important than ethnic similarity (Atkinson, Ponce, & Martinez, 1984). Acculturation status may also determine client responses to treatment (Atkinson, Casa, & Abreu, 1992). "Culture-sensitive" counselors have been rated as being more credible and competent to conduct treatment across cultures by African Americans (Atkinson, Furlong, & Poston, 1986), Asian Americans (Gim, Atkinson, & Kim, 1991), and Mexican Americans (Atkinson, Casa, & Abreu, 1992).

Several authors (for example, Higginbotham, 1979; Sue, Akutsu, & Higashi, 1985; Sue & Zane, 1987; Tseng & McDermott, 1981) have outlined the competencies and knowledge base necessary for therapists to conduct sensitive and effective treatment across cultures. For example, Sue, Akutsu, and Higashi (1985) suggest that the culturally sensitive therapist has acquired (1) knowledge of diverse cultures and lifestyles, (2) skill and comfort in using innovative treatment methods, and (3) actual experience working with culturally diverse clients. It is also critically important for the culturally sensitive therapist to be aware of his or her own cultural background and its influences on definitions and perceptions of abnormal behavior. Furthermore, the therapist must be aware of how cultural beliefs and experiences influence the course of treatment. Comas-Diaz and Jacobsen (1991) have outlined several ways in which ethnocultural factors may shape therapy. These include eliciting strong transference reactions (unconscious projections onto the therapist) and barriers to empathy (understanding of another's experience).

A focus of recent discussions of cross-cultural treatment of abnormal behavior has been culture-specific interventions. Several culture-specific forms of treatment have been identified in the literature, including Naikan and Morita therapy in Japan and espiritismo practiced among some Puerto Ricans. These approaches are generally very "foreign" to many Americans. Naikan therapy, for example, involves a "process of continuous meditation based upon highly structured instruction in self-observation and self-reflection" (Murase, 1986, p. 389). Patients, usually placed in a small sitting area, practice their meditations from early in the morning (about 5:30 A.M.) until the evening (9:00 P.M. or so). Interviewers visit every 90 minutes to discuss progress, usually for about five minutes. Patients are instructed to examine themselves severely, much like a prosecutor would examine an accused prisoner.

Prince (1980) argues that what is common to treatment across cultures is the mobilization of healing forces within the client. Several others (such as Torrey, 1972; Tseng & McDermott, 1981) have also attempted to determine universal features of culture-specific systems of treatment. Although there may well be universal elements underlying systems of cure, culture-specific systems alone appear to address the unique definitions and expressions of abnormal behavior in a given culture.

Conclusion

In this chapter, we have seen that traditional definitions of abnormality may be limited. When the experiences of individuals from other cultures are studied, traditional definitions are not as useful in identifying, assessing, and treating abnormal behavior. There is a continuing controversy about whether to accept universal or culturally relative definitions of abnormal behavior. It seems clear, however, that there are cultural differences in both rates and expressions of major psychological disorders such as schizophrenia and depression. It also seems clear that some forms of abnormal behavior are not universal, but rather are unique to certain cultural settings.

These findings have important implications for psychological adjustment. First, from a health care provider's perspective, recognition of the role of culture in influencing the definition and expression of abnormality is crucial, suggesting that we must modify our methods of assessing and treating abnormal behavior. To develop adequate assessment and treatment strategies, we must take into account knowledge of culturally based definitions of normality and abnormality and culture-specific systems of healing. Research indicates that culturally sensitive assessment and treatment methods are vital to appropriately and effectively meet the mental health needs of culturally diverse populations.

Second, the recognition of the influence of culture on abnormal behavior and psychotherapy is important in our own development of critical thinking skills related to behaviors we may judge as abnormal. Considering cultural factors as a possible mediator of abnormal behavior adds a new and often crucial wrinkle to understanding the behaviors of others, and our own behavior, within the appropriate context in which it developed and is shown. By entertaining the hypothesis that the root of seemingly abnormal behavior is cultural, we allow ourselves to consider how that behavior may indeed be normal when viewed in a different context. Such considerations make it easier to entertain other hypotheses about the causes of normal and abnormal behavior. Improving our critical thinking skills in this fashion enhances our own psychological adjustment.

Glossary

bipolar disorder   A mood disorder characterized by alternating bouts of mania and depression.

catatonia   A form of schizophrenia characterized by extreme withdrawal or agitation.

culture-bound syndromes   Forms of abnormal behavior observed only in certain sociocultural milieus.

depressive disorder   A mood disorder that involves the symptoms of "intense sadness, feelings of futility and worthlessness, and withdrawal from others" (Sue, Sue, & Sue, 1990, p. 325). Depression is often also characterized by physical changes (such as sleep and appetite disturbances) as well as emotional and behavioral changes (Berry et al., 1992).

diathesis-stress model of schizophrenia   A model of schizophrenia that suggests that individuals with a biological predisposition to the disorder (diathesis) may develop the disorder following exposure to environmental stressors.

psychosis   A class of abnormal behavior that is usually characterized by a loss of touch with reality. Psychosis may include delusions or hallucinations.

schizophrenia   Part of a "group of psychotic disorders characterized by gross distortions of reality; withdrawal from social interaction; and disorganization of perception, thought, and emotion" (Carson, Butcher, & Coleman, 1988, p. 322).

statistical-comparison approach   An approach to defining behavior as abnormal as a function of the frequency of its occurrence.

subjective distress   One's individual feelings of distress of negative emotions.

Suggested Readings

Berry, J. W., Poortinga, Y. H., Segall, M. H., & Dasen, P. R. (1992). *Cross-cultural psychology: Research and applications*. New York: Cambridge University Press.

Sue, D., Sue, D., & Sue, S. (1990). *Understanding abnormal behavior* (3rd ed.). Boston: Houghton Mifflin.

Sue, S., & Zane, N. (1987). The role of culture and cultural techniques in psychotherapy: A reformation. *American Psychologist, 42,* 37–45.

Conclusion

Culture itself is invisible, but its influence on our lives is enormous. Culture influences the language we speak, our perceptions of the world around us, our behaviors and attitudes, the structures of our homes, our system of education, our government, and our health. Across the many topics covered in this book, culture plays a major, albeit sometimes silent and invisible, role in determining how we act and how we perceive the actions of others.

When we study cultural differences, it is easy to get lost in the mass of "facts" about those differences. The facts acquired from cross-cultural research in psychology, anthropology, and other disciplines would indeed fill the volumes of an encyclopedia on cultural differences. It would be interesting to have such an encyclopedia—a Farmer's Almanac of Culture, if you will—to help us understand the breadth and scope of culture's influence on our lives.

But even when we are surrounded by all those differences, or perhaps *especially* when we are surrounded by those differences, we must not forget that there are important similarities as well. The study of human behavior across cultures informs us of those similarities as well as the differences. Some processes of perception (for example, of color) are universal, as are some types of cognition and thinking skills and strategies. Processes of language acquisition may be universal, as is the expression of emotions in the face.

Most important, beyond the similarities we find in behaviors, there are important similarities in our underlying intentions, motives, and feelings. When people come together in interaction to form relationships—in business, school, love, and the like—it has been my experience that few people come with malicious intent. Instead, people bring with them good intentions and motives. It is the behavioral manifestations of these intentions and motives, however, that often differ across cultures and that we observe. We get caught up in these differences in the behaviors and forget to think about the underlying intentions of those behaviors. Our nature being what it is, we are most fascinated by differences and often ignore similarities across cultures and among people.

As we learn more and more about both cultural similarities and differences, we need to touch base with the reasons we study cultures in the first place. Without revisiting our motivations, the mass of facts about both similarities and differences will remain just that, a mass of facts. We need a way to take those facts and use them—to allow those facts to become means to an end and not an end in and of themselves. When we revisit our motivations, we should quickly come back to the fact that the ultimate reason we study culture is to improve our lives and our relationships with others in an increasingly diverse world. This goal should be the primary reason we study culture and its influence on human behavior. If we are not able to take the information gathered so far and use it in some productive way, the great opportunity provided by this information will slip through our hands and be wasted.

How can you approach this final task? One way would be to create that *Farmer's Almanac* in your mind, documenting the cultural similarities and differences found in specific cultures and building your own reference title so you can retrieve it at any time. This is a formidable task, as there is so much about culture to learn and so little time, energy, and storage space available. Despite the difficulties, however, this approach is not without merit. Although it might be impossible to gain a deep appreciation of many cultures using this approach, many of us who spend extended periods of time immersed in different cultures—through travels, business, homestay programs, and the like—can and do build this almanac, albeit unconsciously. Moreover, the strength of this approach lies both in increasing our capacity to be culturally relative in relation to others and in guiding our behavior in daily interactions with people from diverse backgrounds.

Guidelines to Improving Cross-Cultural Relationships

In the final section of this chapter, I present seven guidelines I believe will help us improve relationships with others in the future. These guidelines are not universal in the sense that they have been "proven" by cross-cultural research. Instead, they are my feeble attempt at taking all the information presented in this book and my experience and the experiences of others interacting with people of different backgrounds and synthesizing this information into a coherent set of guidelines that I have found useful. Others may have their own guidelines, and those may be at variance with mine. I offer these not as my end-all prescription for successful human relations but as a platform to launch meaningful discussions with others about this important topic. Whether people agree or disagree with these guidelines is a question secondary to the more important issue of their contribution to our ability to talk about these emotionally charged issues.

Recognize That Culture Is a Psychological Construct

I have focused on a definition of culture as a psychological construct emphasizing the subjective (Triandis, 1972) rather than objective aspects of culture. I believe it is these subjective aspects of culture existing in our minds as mental blueprints or programming that are most important to understanding the contribution of culture to human behavior. Culture refers to the degree to which a group of people share attitudes, values, beliefs, and behaviors. It is communicated from one generation to the next. As such, culture is a functional entity—one you cannot see but can only infer from observations of human behavior.

Culture is not race. Being born of a particular race does not mean that you automatically harbor the cultural values associated with that race. Culture is not nationality. Being a citizen of a country does not mean that you automatically adopt the culture associated with that country. Culture is not birthplace. Being born in a certain place does not automatically mean that you harbor the culture of your birthplace.

When we think of intercultural relations and cultural diversity, both within the United States and abroad, we mostly think of differences according to race, ethnicity, or nationality. Yet I have not used these terms and concepts in this book. The lack of a focus on race, ethnicity, and nationality is a function of my view that the important aspect about people is their underlying psychological culture, not the color of their skin or the citizenship on their passport.

Some people may interpret my position as suggesting that race, nationality, and other personal characteristics are not important. That is not true. Future cross-cultural research and thinking in this area must meet the formidable challenge of integrating these concepts with psychological definitions of culture to examine their joint influence and interactive effects on human behaviors. In adopting the approach I took in this book, I hoped to highlight the important role of subjective, psychological culture in producing similarities and differences in behaviors and to bring a fresh way of thinking to old and nagging problems.

As we learn more about what culture is and is not, we need to recognize the fuzzy nature of the definition of culture, based in function rather than biology or geopolitics. By recognizing that culture is a psychological construct—our learned, mental programming—we can avoid the use of race and nationality in understanding cultural differences among people. Defining culture as a meaningful psychological construct also allows us to consider the remaining guidelines.

Recognize Individual Differences within a Culture

Defining culture as a sociopsychological construct is not enough. With a functional definition of culture, we need to recognize individual differences within cultures. Within any culture, people differ according to how strongly they adhere to or comply with the values, standards, and mores of that culture. Whereas some people may be true representatives of their culture, others may not be as adequately described by the culture. Yet they are all members of the culture. Even within our own individualistic American culture we can find people who harbor considerable collectivistic cultural values. Describing all individuals within this cultural group as individualistic ignores actual cultural differences that exist among individual members.

Recognizing that there are individual differences within cultures helps us develop flexibility in our ethnocentrism and stereotypes. One of the keys to improving intergroup and interpersonal relationships is to develop a healthy flexibility with regard to ethnocentrism and stereotypes. Recognizing individual differences in culture and how these differences are related to behaviors is one of the first steps to eliminating reliance on negative and detrimental stereotypes.

Understand Our Own Filters and Ethnocentrism

We are not always aware of our own cultural filters as we perceive, think about, and interpret events around us and the behavior of others. We are not always aware of the cultural bases of our behaviors and actions. Many of the ways we see the world (our worldview) are fundamentally different from the way others see the world.

One important first step in gaining an understanding of cultural influences on behavior is to recognize that we have our own filters for perception and bases for behavior. We need to stop and think about how our own cultural upbringing contributes to how we interact with the world and with others. One arena where this comparison comes to the forefront is when we travel outside our culture. By clashing with the cultures of others, we are forced to think about differences in cognition and behavior. In doing so, we may come to a better understanding of our own filters and biases.

Allow for the Possibility That Conflicts Are Cultural

One fallacy that exists in cross-cultural study is the assumption that if you study cultures, there will be no intercultural conflicts. This is not the case. In interacting with others, conflicts and misunderstandings will undoubtedly occur. Unfortunately, all too often we are too quick to attribute the cause of the conflict or misunderstanding to some kind of fault or shortcoming in the other person or with the other person's culture. Often, because we have a limited understanding of culture based on race or nationality, we make negative attributions about that race or nationality, when in fact the differences arose because of culture, not race or nationality.

With a better understanding of cultural influences on behavior, we can allow for the possibility that many conflicts and misunderstandings are due to cultural differences. By doing so, we avoid personalizing the source of conflict and misunderstanding in our interactions and focus on the reasons the misunderstanding may have arisen in the first place. Of course, some conflicts do arise because of personal differences, ignorance, stupidity, or close-mindedness. But we can allow that culture may be a contributing factor and give people the benefit of the doubt.

Recognize That Cultural Differences Are Legitimate

Simply allowing for conflicts and misunderstandings to be attributed to culture is not enough. Indeed, we need to recognize and respect legitimate differences between our cultural upbringing and that of others. This is often a very difficult task because our perception of transgressions to our own culturally appropriate ways of behaving are typically seen as "bad" or "wrong" in our own cultural context, and it is easy to label the same behaviors of others as "bad" or "wrong." But a person from another culture may view those same behaviors as "good" or "acceptable" or "normal." In fact, behaviors that seem bad or ignorant or stupid to us may in fact be performed by a person of sincerity and trustworthiness. No matter how much we want to label it as bad or ignorant or stupid, the other person's cultural ways and values and beliefs have just as much legitimacy to them as ours have to us. A step in the right direction is to respect that legitimacy and that difference and find a way to work from that level of respect.

Have Tolerance, Be Patient, and Presume Good Intent

How can we find ways to work things out? Where do we go, once we recognize that conflicts arise because of differences in culture and that cultural differences in others are legitimate? One answer lies in examining how we traditionally deal with these conflicts.

American culture is based on a considerable amount of preservation of an individualistic sense of self. In finding ways to maintain self-integrity, we unfortunately often attribute negative characteristics to others, lashing out at others immediately when we feel our cultural norms have been violated. This style of making attributions and understanding the world around us is related to our individualistic American culture. It is neither bad nor good; it is just the way things are.

When we are too quick to attribute negative characteristics to others, we deny the possibility that their intent may have been good and that it was only the behavioral manifestations of that good intent that we were at odds with. By being tolerant of transgressions and presuming good intent in intercultural interaction, we allow that possibility to exist. If all participants of that interaction practice tolerance and presume good intent, we will be able to operate on the level of psychological culture discussed throughout this book and find ways to explore and react to underlying intent, rather than focusing solely on behaviors we find offensive.

Learn More about Cultural Influences on Behavior

As we turn toward the future, we must continue to learn how culture influences human behavior. By recognizing the importance of culture on behavior, we face an incredible challenge and opportunity. The diverse world that faces us, not only in the United States but also relative to our interdependence on others in our global village, provides a rich and complex arena for human behavior. Psychology has yet to explore this arena fully. These challenges bring new opportunities and new hopes, not only for science but also for people and their lives.

As we come in contact with people of different cultures from around the world, either through our own travels or through theirs, we are exposed to many different ways culture manifests itself in behavior. As our understanding grows, we will come to appreciate even more the important role culture plays, not only in providing us with a way to live but also in helping us meet the challenges of survival successfully and with integrity. Changes in culture will continue to occur; culture is not a static, fixed entity. We know that cultures change over time; the changes we witness today in Europe, Russia, Asia, and even within our own country speak to this fact. These changes ensure that there will never be a shortage of things to learn about cultural influences on human behavior. The important thing is that we have to want to learn it.

In Knowing Others, We Will Come to Know Ourselves

I hope I have been able to convey to you that human behavior is too rich and complex to be "captured" by understanding the world through the eyes of a single culture. One of the major goals of this book has been to examine how culture influences our behaviors and our lives and to challenge the many truths of our cultural world. Many cross-cultural studies in the literature speak to this breadth, and to this need.

In challenging the "traditional," we cannot and should not disregard its importance or the work that produced that knowledge. Indeed, to disregard that material or the work that produced it would be insensitive, and that has no place in academic work. But we have much more to learn, and as time progresses the need to learn increases. Improvements in communications technologies bring previously distant points on the globe closer and closer together to further enmesh us in the global village. The opening of national borders and the infusion of people from all walks of life and cultures in our workplaces and in our families ensures that cross-cultural issues will remain a high priority in the years to come.

Can we keep up? Further cross-cultural research will help uncover universal and culture-specific aspects of human behavior. Scholars will increasingly have to include culture as a major determinant in theories of human behavior, and researchers will include culture as a variable in their studies. As new information is uncovered, we will undoubtedly improve our thinking about the nature of culture and cultural influences on the behavior of others. In knowing others, we will eventually come to know ourselves.

References

Abebimpe, V. R. (1981). Overview: White norms and psychiatric diagnosis of black patients. *American Journal of Psychiatry, 139*, 888–891.

Albright, L., Kenny, D. A., & Malloy, T. E. (1988). Consensus in personality judgements at zero acquaintance. *Journal of Personality and Social Psychology, 55*, 387–395.

Allen, L., & Santrock, J. W. (1993). *Psychology: The context of behavior.* Dubuque, IA: Brown & Benchmark.

Altman, S. A. (1962). A field study of the sociobiology of rhesus monkeys, *Macacca mulatta. Annals of the New York Academy of Sciences, 102*, 338–435.

American Psychiatric Association. (1987). *Diagnostic and statistical manual of mental disorders* (3rd ed.) [DSM-III-R]. Washington, DC: APA.

Archer, D. (Producer and director). (1991). *A world of gestures: Culture and nonverbal communication* [Videotape]. Berkeley: University of California Extension Center for Media and Independent Learning.

Argyle, M., & Cook, M. (1976). *Gaze and mutual gaze.* Cambridge, England: Cambridge University Press.

Argyle, M., Henderson, M., Bond, M. H., Iizuka, Y., & Contarello, A. (1986). Cross-cultural variations in relationship rules. *International Journal of Psychology, 21*, 287–315.

Asch, S. E. (1951). Effects of group pressure upon the modification and distortion of judgments. In H. Guetzkow (Ed.), *Groups, leadership and men: Research in human relations* (pp. 177–190). Pittsburgh: Carnegie Press.

Asch, S. E. (1955). Opinions and social pressures. *Scientific American, 193*, 31–35.

Asch, S. E. (1956). Studies of independence and conformity: A minority of one against a unanimous majority. *Psychological Monographs, 70* (9, Whole No. 416).

Atkinson, D. R., Casa, A., & Abreu, J. (1992). Mexican American acculturation, counselor ethnicity and cultural sensitivity, and perceived counselor competence. *American Psychologist, 39*, 515–520.

Atkinson, D. R., Furlong, M. J., & Poston, W. C. (1986). Afro-American preferences for counselor characteristics. *Journal of Counseling Psychology, 33*, 326–330.

Atkinson, D. R., Ponce, F. Q., & Martinez, F. M. (1984). Effects of ethnic, sex, and attitude similarity on counselor credibility. *Journal of Counseling Psychology, 31*, 588–590.

Atkinson, J. W. (1964). *An introduction to motivation*. Princeton, NJ: Van Nostrand.

Barnouw, V. (1985). *Culture and personality*. Chicago: Dorsey Press.

Barry, H., Josephson, L., Lauer, E., & Marshall, C. (1976). Agents and techniques for child training. *Ethnology, 16*, 191–230.

Beiser, M. (1985). A study of depression among traditional Africans, urban North Americans, and Southeast Asian refugees. In A. Kleinman & B. Good (Eds.), *Culture and depression: Studies in the anthropology and cross-cultural psychiatry of affect and disorder* (pp. 272–298). Berkeley: University of California Press.

Benedict, R. (1946). *The chrysanthemum and the sword*. Boston: Houghton Mifflin.

Berkman, L. F., & Syme, S. L. (1979). Social networks, host resistance, and mortality: A nine-year follow-up study of Alameda County residents. *American Journal of Epidemiology, 109*, 186–204.

Berry, D. S., & McArthur, L. Z. (1985). Some components and consequences of a babyface. *Journal of Personality and Social Psychology, 48*, 312–323.

Berry, D. S., & McArthur, L. Z. (1986). Perceiving character in faces: The impact of age-related craniofacial changes in social perception. *Psychological Bulletin, 100*, 3–18.

Berry, J. W. (1966). Temne and Eskimo perceptual skills. *International Journal of Psychology, 1*, 207–229.

Berry, J. W. (1976). Sex differences in behavior and cultural complexity. *Indian Journal of Psychology, 51*, 89–97.

Berry, J. W., Poortinga, Y. H., Segall, M., & Dasen, P. R. (1992). *Cross-cultural psychology: Research and applications*. Cambridge: Cambridge University Press.

Berscheid, E., & Walster, E. (1978). *Interpersonal attraction*. Reading, MA: Addison-Wesley.

Block, J. (1983). Differential premises arising from differential socialization of the sexes: Some conjectures. *Child Development, 54*, 1335–1354.

Bond, M. H. (1986). *The psychology of the Chinese people*. New York: Oxford University Press.

Bond, M. H., & Forgas, J. P. (1984). Linking person perception to behavior intention across cultures: The role of cultural collectivism. *Journal of Cross-Cultural Psychology, 15*, 337–352.

Bond, M. H., & Tak-Sing, C. (1983). College students' spontaneous self-concept: The effect of culture among respondents in Hong Kong, Japan, and the United States. *Journal of Cross-cultural Psychology, 14*, 153–171.

Born, M., Bleichrodt, N., & Van der Flier, H. (1987). Cross-cultural comparison of sex-related differences on intelligence tests: A meta-analysis. *Journal of Cross-Cultural Psychology, 18*, 283–314.

Brehm, S. S. (1985). *Intimate relationships*. New York: Random House.

Brewer, M. B., & Kramer, R. M. (1985). The psychology of intergroup attitudes and behavior. *Annual Review of Psychology, 36*, 219–243.

Brislin, R. (1993). *Understanding culture's influence on behavior*. Fort Worth, TX: Harcourt Brace Jovanovich.

Buck, E. B., Newton, B. J., & Muramatsu, Y. (1984). Independence and obedience in the U.S. and Japan. *International Journal of Intercultural Relations, 8*, 279–300.

Burgos, N. M., & Diaz-Perez, Y. I. (1986). An explanation of human sexuality in the Puerto Rican culture. [Special issue: *Human sexuality, ethnoculture, and social work.*] *Journal of Social Work and Human Sexuality, 4*, 135–150.

Buss, D. M. (1988). The evolution of human intrasexual competition: Tactics of mate attraction. *Journal of Personality and Social Psychology, 54*, 616–628.

Buss, D. M. (1989). Sex differences in human mate preferences: Evolutionary hypotheses tested in 37 cultures. *Behavioral and Brain Sciences, 12*, 1–49.

Calhoun, J. B. (1950). The study of wild animals under controlled conditions. *Annals of the New York Academy of Sciences, 51*, 113–122.

Carson, R. C., Butcher, J. N., & Coleman, J. C. (1988). *Abnormal psychology and modern life* (8th ed.). Glenview, IL: Scott, Foresman.

Cashmore, J. A., & Goodnow, J. J. (1986). Influences on Australian parents' values: Ethnicity versus sociometric status.

Journal of Cross-Cultural Psychology, 17, 441–454.

Chinese Culture Connection. (1987). Chinese values and the search for culture-free dimensions of culture. *Journal of Cross-Cultural Psychology, 18,* 143–164.

Collett, P. (1971). On training Englishmen in the non-verbal behavior of Arabs: An experiment in inter-cultural communication. *International Journal of Psychology, 6,* 209–215.

Comas-Diaz, L. (1992). The future of psychotherapy with ethnic minorities *Psychotherapy, 29,* 88–94.

Comas-Diaz, L., & Jacobsen, F. M. (1991). Ethnocultural transference and countertransference in the therapeutic dyad. *American Journal of Orthopsychiatry, 61,* 392–402.

Cousins, S. D. (1989). Culture and self-perception in Japan and the United States. *Journal of Personality and Social Psychology, 56,* 124–131.

Deck, L. P. (1968). Buying brains by the inch. *Journal of College and University Personnel Associations, 19,* 33–37.

DePaulo, B. M., Stone, J., & Lassiter, G. D. (1985). Deceiving and detecting deceit. In B. R. Schlenker (Ed.), *The self and social life* (pp. 323–370). New York: McGraw-Hill.

Dion, K. K. (1986). Stereotyping based on physical attractiveness: Issues and conceptual perspectives. In C. P. Herman, M. P. Zanna, & E. T. Higgins (Eds.), *Ontario symposium on personality and social psychology* (Vol. 3). Hillsdale, NJ: Erlbaum.

Doi K. (1982). Two-dimensional theory of achievement motivation. *Japanese Journal of Psychology, 52,* 344–350.

Doi, K. (1985). The relation between the two dimensions of achievement motivation and personality of male university students. *Japanese Journal of Psychology, 56,* 107–110.

Earley, P. C. (1989). Social loafing and collectivism: A comparison of the United States and the People's Republic of China. *Administrative Science Quarterly, 34,* 565–581.

Ekman, P., Friesen, W. V., & Bear, J. (1984, May). International language of gestures. *Psychology Today,* pp. 64–69.

Ekman, P., Levenson, R., & Friesen, W. V. (1983). Autonomic nervous system activity distinguishes among emotions. *Science, 221,* 1208–1210.

El-Islam, M. F. (1983). Cultural change and intergenerational relationships in Arabian families. *International Journal of Family Psychiatry, 4,* 321–329.

Espin, O. M. (1993). Feminist theory: Not for or by white women only. *Counseling Psychologist, 21,* 103–108.

Exline, R. V., Jones, P., & Maciorowski, K. (1977). *Race, affiliative-conflict theory and mutual visual attention during conversation.* Paper presented at the American Psychological Association meeting in San Francisco.

Fehr, B. J. (1977). *Visual interactions in same and interracial dyads.* Unpublished master's thesis, University of Delaware.

Fehr, B. J. (1981). *The communication of evaluation through the use of interpersonal gaze in same and interracial female dyads.* Unpublished doctoral dissertation, University of Delaware.

Fehr, B. J., & Exline, R. V. (1987). Social visual interaction: A conceptual and literature review. In A. W. Siegman & S. Feldstein (Eds.), *Nonverbal behavior and communication* (2nd ed.) (pp. 225–326). Hillsdale, NJ: Erlbaum.

Feist, J., & Brannon, L. (1988). *Health psychology: An introduction to behavior and health.* Belmont, CA: Wadsworth.

Ferrante, J. (1992). *Sociology: A global perspective.* Belmont, CA: Wadsworth.

Festinger, L., Schachter, S., & Back, K. (1950). *Social pressures in informal groups: A study of human factors in housing.* New York: Harper.

Forston, R. F., & Larson, C. U. (1968). The dynamics of space: An experimental study in proxemic behavior among Latin Americans and North Americans. *Journal of Communication, 18,* 109–116.

Friedman, M., & Rosenman, R. H. (1974). *Type A behavior and your heart.* New York: Knopf.

Furnham, A. F. (1984). Value systems and anomie in three cultures. *International Journal of Psychology, 19,* 565–579.

Gabrenya, W. K., Jr., Wang, Y., & Latane, B. (1985). Social loafing on an optimizing task: Cross-cultural differences among Chinese and Americans. *Journal of Cross-Cultural Psychology, 16,* 223–242.

Garratt, G. A., Baxter, J. C., & Rozelle, R. M. (1981). Training university police in black-American nonverbal behaviors. *Journal of Social Psychology, 113,* 217–229.

Geertz, C. (1975). From the natives' point of view: On the nature of anthropological understanding. *American Scientist, 63,* 47–53.

Gilligan, C. (1982). *In a different voice: Psychological theory and women's development.* Cambridge, MA: Harvard University Press.

Gim, R. H., Atkinson, D. R., & Kim, S. J. (1991). Asian-American acculturation, counselor ethnicity and cultural sensitivity, and ratings of counselors. *Journal of Counseling Psychology, 38,* 57–62.

Hadiyono, J. E. P., & Hahn, M. W. (1985). Personality differences and sex similarities in American and Indonesian college students. *Journal of Social Psychology, 125,* 703–708.

Hall, C. C. I., Evans, B. J., & Selice, S. (Eds.). (1989). *Black females in the United States: A bibliography from 1967 to 1987.* Washington, DC: American Psychological Association.

Hall, E. T. (1963). A system for the notation of proxemic behavior. *American Anthropologist, 65,* 1003–1026.

Hall, E. T. (1966). *The hidden dimension.* New York: Doubleday.

Hall, J. A. (1978). Gender effects in decoding nonverbal cues. *Psychological Bulletin, 85,* 845–857.

Hall, K. R. L., & Devore, I. (1965). Baboon social behavior. In I. Devore (Ed.), *Primate behavior.* New York: Holt, Rinehart & Winston.

Harkins, S. G. (1987). Social loafing and social facilitation. *Journal of Experimental Social Psychology, 23,* 1–18.

Harkins, S. G., & Petty, R. E. (1982). Effects of task difficulty and task uniqueness on social loafing. *Journal of Personality and Social Psychology, 43,* 1214–1229.

Hatfield, E. (1988). Passionate and companionate love. In R. J. Sternberg & M. L. Barnes (Eds.), *The psychology of love* (pp. 191–217). New Haven, CT: Yale University Press.

Hendrick, C., & Hendrick, S. (1983). *Liking, loving, and relating.* Pacific Grove, CA: Brooks/Cole.

Higginbotham, H. N. (1979). Culture and mental health services. In A. J. Marsella, G. DeVos, & F. L. K. Hsu (Eds.), *Perspectives on cross-cultural psychology* (pp. 307–332). New York: Academic Press.

Hinde, R. A., & Rowell, T. E. (1962). Communication by posture and facial expressions in the rhesus monkey (*Macaca mulatta*). *Proceedings of the Zoological Society of London, 138,* 1–21.

Hofstede, G. (1980). *Culture's consequences: International differences in work-related values.* Newbury Park, CA: Sage.

Hofstede, G. (1983). Dimensions of national cultures in fifty countries and three regions. In J. B. Deregowski, S. Dziurawiec, & R. C. Annis (Eds.), *Expiscations in cross-cultural psychology* (pp. 335–355). Lisse: Swets & Zeitlinger.

Hofstede, G. (1984). *Culture's consequences: International differences in work-related values.* Newbury Park, CA: Sage.

Hofstede, G., & Bond, M. (1988). Confucius & economic growth: New trends in culture's consequences. *Organizational Dynamics, 16*(4), 4–21.

Huang, L. N., & Ying, Y. (1989). Japanese children and adolescents. In J. T. Gibbs & L. N. Huang (Eds.), *Children of color.* San Francisco: Jossey-Bass.

Ineichen, B. (1979). The social geography of marriage. In M. Cook & G. Wilson (Eds.), *Love and attraction.* New York: Pergamon Press.

Jackson, J. M., & Williams, K. D. (1985). Social loafing on difficult tasks: Working collectively can improve performance. *Journal of Personality and Social Psychology, 49,* 937–942.

James, W. (1890). *The principles of psychology* (Vols. 1 and 2). New York: Holt.

Jones, E. E., & Harris, V. A. (1967). The attribution of attitudes. *Journal of Experimental Social Psychology, 3,* 1–24.

Joseph, R. A., Markus, H. R., & Tafarodi, R. W. (1992). Gender differences in the source of self-esteem. *Journal of Personality and Social Psychology, 63,* 1017–1028.

Karno, M., Jenkins, J. H., De la Selva, A., Santana, F., Telles, C., Lopez, S., & Mintz, J. (1987). Expressed emotion and schizophrenic outcome among Mexican-American families. *Journal of Nervous and Mental Disease, 175,* 145–151.

Kendon, A. (1987). On gesture: Its complementary relationship with speech. In A. W. Siegman & S. Feldstein (Eds.), *Nonverbal behavior and communication* (pp. 65–97). Hillsdale, NJ: Erlbaum.

Kiev, A. (1972). *Transcultural psychiatry.* New York: Free Press.

Kitayama, S., & Markus, H. R. (in press, a). A cultural perspective to self-conscious emotions. In J. P. Tangney & K. Fisher (Eds.), *Shame, guilt, embarrassment, and pride: Empirical studies of self-conscious emotions.* New York: Guilford Press.

Kitayama, S., & Markus, H. R. (in press, b). Culture and self: Implications for internationalizing psychology. In J. D'Arms, R. G. Hastie, & H. K. Jacobson (Eds.), *Becoming more international and global: Challenges for American higher education.* Ann Arbor: University of Michigan Press.

Kitayama, S., Markus, H. R., Kurokawa, M., & Negishi, K. (1993). *Social orientation of emotions: Cross-cultural evidence and implications.* Unpublished manuscript. University of Oregon.

Kleinman, A. (1978). Culture and depression. *Culture and Medical Psychiatry, 2,* 295–296.

Kleinman, A. (1988). *Rethinking psychiatry: From cultural category to personal experience.* New York: Free Press.

Kluckholn, F., & Strodtbeck, F. (1961). *Variations in value orientations.* Evanston, IL: Row, Peterson.

LaFrance, M., & Mayo, C. (1976). Racial differences in gaze behavior during conversations: Two systematic observational studies. *Journal of Personality and Social Psychology, 33*(5), 547–552.

Latane, B. (1981). The psychology of social impact. *American Psychologist, 36,* 343–356.

Latane, B., Williams, K., & Harkins, S. (1979). Many hands make light the work: The causes and consequences of social loafing. *Journal of Personality and Social Psychology, 37,* 322–332.

Laurent, A. (1978). *Matrix organizations and Latin cultures.* Working Paper 78-28. Brussels: European Institute for Advanced Studies in Management.

Leff, J. (1977). International variations in the diagnosis of psychiatric illness. *British Journal of Psychiatry, 131,* 329–338.

Leff, J. (1981). *Psychiatry around the globe: A transcultural view.* New York: Marcel Dekker.

Leff, J. (1986). The epidemiology of mental illness. In J. L. Cox (Ed)., *Transcultural psychiatry* (pp. 23–36). London: Croom Helm.

Lively, W. J., & Bromley, D. B. (1973). *Person perception in childhood and adolescence.* London: Wiley.

Lonner, W. J., & Ibrahim, F. A. (1989). Assessment in cross-cultural counseling. In P. B. Pedersen, J. Dragus, W. Lonner, & J. E. Trimble (Eds.), *Counseling across cultures* (3rd ed.) (pp. 299–334). Honolulu: University of Hawaii Press.

Maccoby, E. E., & Jacklin, C. N. (1974). *The psychology of sex differences.* Stanford, CA: Stanford University Press.

Maehr, M., & Nicholls, J. (1980). Culture and achievement motivation: A second look. In N. Warren (Ed.), *Studies in cross-cultural psychology* (Vol. 2, pp. 221–267). London: Academic Press.

Manson, S. M., & Shore, J. H. (1981). Psychiatric epidemological research among American Indian and Alaska Natives: Some methodological issues. *White Cloud Journal, 2,* 48–56.

Manson, S. M., Shore, J. H., & Bloom, J. D. (1985). The depressive experience in American Indian communities: A challenge for psychiatric theory and diagnosis. In A. Kleinman & B. Good (Eds.), *Culture and depression: Studies in the anthropology and cross-cultural psychiatry of affect and disorder* (pp. 331–368). Berkeley: University of California Press.

Markus, H. R. (1977). Self-schemata and processing information about the self. *Journal of Personality and Social Psychology, 35,* 63–78.

Markus, H. R., & Kitayama, S. (1991a). Culture and the self: Implications for cognition, emotion, and motivation. *Psychological Review, 98,* 224–253.

Markus, H. R., & Kitayama, S. (1991b). Cultural variation in self-concept. In G. R. Goethals & J. Strauss (Eds.), *Multidisciplinary perspectives on the self.* New York: Springer-Verlag.

Marmot, M. G., & Syme, S. L (1976). Acculturation and coronary heart disease in Japanese Americans. *American Journal of Epidemiology, 104,* 225–247.

Marsella, A. J. (1979). Cross-cultural studies of mental disorders. In A. J. Marsella, G. DeVos, & F. L. K. Hsu (Eds.), *Perspectives on cross-cultural psychology* (pp. 233–262). New York: Academic Press.

Marsella, A. J. (1980). Depressive experience and disorder across cultures. In H. C. Triandis & J. Dragus (Eds.), *Handbook of cross-cultural psychology. Vol. 6, Psychopathology* (pp. 237–289). Boston: Allyn & Bacon.

Matsumoto, D. (1991). Cultural influences on facial expressions of emotion. *Southern Communication Journal, 56,* 128–137.

Matsumoto, D., & Fletcher, D. (1996). Cultural influences on disease. *Journal of Gender, Culture, and Health, 1,* 71-82.

Matsumoto, D., & Kudoh, T. (1993). American-Japanese cultural differences in attributions of personality based on smiles. *Journal of Nonverbal Behavior, 17*(4), 231–243.

Matsumoto, D., Pun, K. K., Nakatani, M., Kadowaki, D., Weissman, M., McCarter, L., Fletcher, D., & Takeuchi, S. (1995). Cultural differences in attitudes and concerns about osteoporosis in older Japanese and Japanese-American women: Differential implications for patient management. *Women and Health, 23,* 39-56.

McClelland, D. C. (1961). *The achieving society.* Princeton, NJ: Van Nostrand.

Mead, M. (1961). *Cooperation and competition among primitive people.* Boston: Beacon Press.

Mehrabian, A. (1981). *Silent messages: Implications of emotions and attitudes* (2nd ed.). Belmont, CA: Wadsworth.

Messick, D. M., & Mackie, D. M. (1989). Intergroup relations. *Annual Review of Psychology, 40,* 45–81.

Milgram, S. (1963). Behavioral study of obedience. *Journal of Abnormal and Social Psychology, 67,* 371–378.

Milgram, S. (1964). Issues in the study of obedience. *American Psychologist, 19,* 848–852.

Milgram, S. (1974). *Obedience to authority.* New York: Harper & Row.

Miller, J. G. (1984). Culture and the development of everyday social explanation. *Journal of Personality and Social Psychology, 46,* 961–978.

Mintz, J., Mintz, L., & Goldstein, M. (1987). Expressed emotion and relapse in first episodes of schizophrenia. *British Journal of Psychiatry, 151,* 314–320.

Morris, D., Collett, P., Marsh, P., & O'Shaughnessy, M. (1980). *Gestures: Their origins and distribution.* New York: Scarborough.

Murase, T. (1986). Naikan therapy. In T. S. Lebra & W. P. Lebra (Eds.), *Japanese culture and behavior* (pp. 388–398). Honolulu: University of Hawaii Press.

Murphy, H. B. M. (1982). Culture and schizophrenia. In I. Al-Issa (Ed.), *Culture and psychopathology* (pp. 221–249), Baltimore, MD: University Park Press.

Murphy, J. M. (1976). Psychiatric labeling in cross-cultural perspective. *Science, 191,* 1019–1028.

Myers, D. (1987). *Social psychology* (2nd ed.). New York: McGraw-Hill.

Myers, J. K., Weissman, M. M., Tischler, G. L., Holzer, C. E., Leaf, P. J., Orvaschel, H., Anthony, J. C., Boyd, J. H., Burke, J. D., Kramer, M., & Stolzman, R. (1984). Six-month prevalence of psychiatric disorders in three communities: 1980 to 1982. *Archives of General Psychiatry, 41,* 959–967.

Noesjirwan, J. (1977). Contrasting cultural patterns of interpersonal closeness in doctors' waiting rooms in Sydney and Jakarta. *Journal of Cross-Cultural Psychology, 8,* 357–368.

Noesjirwan, J. (1978). A laboratory study of proxemic patterns of Indonesians and Australians. *British Journal of Social and Clinical Psychology, 17,* 333–334.

Okamoto, K. (1993). *Nihonjin no YES wa Naze No Ka? (Why is a Japanese yes a no?).* Toyko, Japan: PHP Research Laboratory.

Opler, M. K., & Singer, J. L. (1959). Ethnic differences in behavior and psychopathology. *International Journal of Social Psychiatry, 2*, 11–23.

Patzer, G. L. (1985). *The physical attractiveness phenomena.* New York: Plenum Press.

Pfeiffer, W. M. (1982). Culture-bound syndromes. In I. Al-Issa (Ed.), *Culture and psychopathology* (pp. 201–218). Baltimore, MD: University Park Press.

Piaget, J. (1952). *The origins of intelligence in children.* New York: International Universities Press.

Piaget, J. (1954). *The construction of reality in the child.* New York: Basic Books.

Prince, R. (1980). Variations in psychotherapeutic procedures. In H. C. Triandis & J. Dragus (Eds.), *Handbook of cross-cultural psychology. Vol. 6, Psychopathology* (pp. 291–349). Boston: Allyn & Bacon.

Punetha, D., Giles, H., & Young, L. (1987). Ethnicity and immigrant values: Religion and language choice. *Journal of Language and Social Psychology, 6*, 229–241.

Robins, L. N., Helzer, J. E., Weissman, M. M., Orvaschel, H., Gruenberg, E., Burke, J. D., & Reiger, D. (1984). Lifetime prevalence of specific psychiatric disorders in three sites. *Archives of General Psychiatry, 41*, 949–958.

Roemer, M. I. (1993). *National health systems of the world: The issues* (Vol. 2). New York: Oxford University Press.

Ross, J., & Ferris, K. R. (1981). Interpersonal attraction and organizational outcome: A field experiment. *Administrative Science Quarterly, 26*, 617–632.

Ross, L. (1977). The intuitive psychologist and his shortcomings: Distortions in the attribution process. In L. Berkowitz (Ed.), *Advances in experimental social psychology* (Vol. 10, pp. 174–221). New York: Academic Press.

Ryan, R. A. (1980). Strengths of the American Indian family: State of the art. In F. Hoffman (Ed.), *The American Indian family: Strength and stresses.* Isleta, NM: American Indian Social Research and Development Association.

Schaller, G. (1963). *The mountain gorilla.* Chicago: University of Chicago Press.

Schaller, G. (1964). *The year of the gorilla.* Chicago: University of Chicago Press.

Segall, M. H., Dasen, P. R., Berry, J. W., & Poortinga, Y. H. (1990). *Human behavior in global perspective: An introduction to cross-cultural psychology.* New York: Pergamon Press.

Shepperd, J., & Wright, R. (1989). Individual contributions to a collective effort: An incentive analysis. *Personality and Social Psychology Bulletin, 15*, 141–149.

Shirakashi, S. (1985). Social loafing of Japanese students. *Hiroshima Forum for Psychology, 10*, 35–40.

Shuter, R. (1976). Proxemics and tactility in Latin America. *Journal of Communication, 26*, 46–52.

Shuter, R. (1977). A field study of nonverbal communication in Germany, Italy, and the United States. *Communication Monographs, 44*, 298–305.

Shweder, R. A., & Bourne, E. J. (1984). Does the concept of the person vary cross-culturally? In R. A. Shweder & R. A. LeVine (Eds.), *Culture theory: Essays on mind, self, and emotion* (pp. 158–199). Cambridge, England: Cambridge University Press.

Simmons, C. H., vomKolke, A., & Shimizu, H. (1986). Attitudes toward romantic love among American, German and Japanese students. *Journal of Social Psychology, 126*, 327–336.

Simonds, P. E. (1965). The bonnet macaque in South India. In I. DeVore (Ed.), *Primate behavior: Field studies of monkeys and apes* (pp. 175–196). New York: Holt, Rinehart & Winston.

Sternberg, R. J. (1988). Triangulating love. In R. J. Sternberg & M. L. Barnes (Eds.), *The psychology of love* (pp. 119–138). New Haven, CT: Yale University Press.

Stropes-Roe, M., & Cochrane, R. (1990). The child-rearing values of Asian and British parents and young people: An inter-ethnic and inter-generational comparison in the evolution of Kohn's 13 qualities. *British Journal of Social Psychology, 29*, 149–160.

Stryker, S. (1986). Identity theory: Developments and extensions. In K. Tardley & T. Honess (Eds.), *Self and identity* (pp. 89–107). New York: John Wiley.

Sue, D., Sue, D., & Sue, S. (1990). *Understanding abnormal behavior* (3rd ed.). Boston: Houghton Mifflin.

Sue, S. (1977). Community mental health services to minority groups: Some optimism, some pessimism. *American Psychologist, 32,* 616–624.

Sue, S. (1989). Foreword. In J. T. Gibbs & L. N. Huang (Eds.), *Children of color.* San Francisco: Jossey-Bass.

Sue, S. (1991, August). *Ethnicity and mental health: Research and policy issues.* Invited address presented at the Annual Meeting of the American Psychological Association, San Francisco, CA.

Sue, S., Akutsu, P. O., & Higashi, C. (1985). Training issues in conducting therapy with ethnic minority group clients. In P. Pedersen (Ed.), *Handbook of cross-cultural counseling and therapy* (pp. 275–280). Westport, CT: Greenwood.

Sue, S., & Morishima, J. K. (1982). *The mental health of Asian Americans.* San Francisco: Jossey-Bass.

Sue, S., & Zane, N. (1987). The role of culture and cultural techniques in psychotherapy: A reformation. *American Psychologist, 42,* 37–45.

Swartz, L. (1985). Anorexia nervosa as a culture-bound syndrome. *Social Science and Medicine, 20,* 725–730.

Tajfel, H. (1982). Social psychology of intergroup relations. *Annual Review of Psychology, 33,* 1–39.

Terrell, M. D. (1992, August). *Stress, coping, ethnic identity and college adjustment.* Paper presented at the Annual Meeting of the American Psychological Association, Washington, DC.

Thomas, A., & Sillen, S. (1972). *Racism and psychiatry.* New York: Brunner/Mazel.

Ting-Toomey, S. (1991). Intimacy expressions in three cultures: France, Japan, and the United States. *International Journal of Intercultural Relations, 15,* 29–46.

Torrey, E. F. (1972). *The mind game: Witchdoctors and psychiatrists.* New York: Emerson Hall.

Triandis, H. C. (1972). *The analysis of subjective culture.* New York: Wiley.

Triandis, H. C. (1989). The self and social behavior in differing cultural contexts. *Psychological Review, 96,* 506–520.

Triandis, H. C. (1992, February). *Individualism and collectivism as a cultural syndrome.* Paper presented at the Annual Convention of the Society for Cross-Cultural Researchers, Santa Fe, NM.

Triandis, H. C., Bontempo, R., Villareal, M. J., Asai, M., & Lucca, N. (1988). Individualism and collectivism: Cross-cultural perspectives on self-ingroup relationships. *Journal of Personality and Social Psychology, 4,* 323–338.

Tseng, W., & McDermott, J. F. (1981). *Culture, mind and therapy: An introduction to cultural psychiatry.* New York: Brunner/Mazel.

van Hooff, J. A. R. A. M. (1967). The facial displays of the catarrhine monkeys and apes. In D. Morris (Ed.), *Primate ethology* (pp. 7–68). London: Weidenfeld and Nicolson.

Watson, O. M. (1970). *Proxemic behavior: A cross-cultural study.* The Hague: Mouton.

Watson, O. M., & Graves, T. D. (1966). Quantitative research in proxemic behavior. *American Anthropologist, 68,* 971–985.

Weldon, E., & Gargano, G. M. (1988). Cognitive loafing: The effects of accountability and shared responsibility on cognitive effort. *Personality and Social Psychology Bulletin, 14,* 159–171.

Wierzbicka, A. (1986). Human emotions: Universal or culture-specific? *American Anthropologist, 88,* 584–594.

Williams, J., & Best, D. (1982). *Measuring sex stereotypes: A thirty-nation study.* Newbury Park, CA: Sage.

Williams, J., & Best, D. (1990). *Measuring sex stereotypes: A multination study.* Newbury Park, CA: Sage.

Williams, J., & Best, D. (1994). Cross-cultural views of women and men. In W. Lonner & R. Malpass (Eds.), *Psychology and culture.* Boston: Allyn & Bacon.

World Health Organization. (1973). *Report of the International Pilot Study of Schizophrenia* (Vol. 1). Geneva: WHO.

World Health Organization. (1979). *Schizophrenia: An international follow-up study.* New York: John Wiley.

World Health Organization. (1981). *Current state of diagnosis and classification in the mental health field.* Geneva: WHO.

World Health Organization. (1991). *World health statistics quarterly*. Geneva: WHO.

Wylie, R. C. (1979). *The self concept, Vol. 2: Theory and research on selected topics*. Lincoln: University of Nebraska Press.

Yamaguchi, S., Okamoto, K., & Oka, T. (1985). Effects of coactor's presence: Social loafing and social facilitation. *Japanese Psychological Research, 27*, 215–222.

Yang, K. S. (1982). Causal attributions of academic success and failure and their affective consequences. *Chinese Journal of Psychology* [Taiwan], *24*, 65–83. (The abstract only is in English.)

Yap, P. M. (1974). *Comparative psychiatry. A theoretical framework*. Toronto: University of Toronto Press.

Yu, E. S. H. (1974). Achievement motive, familism, and hsiao: A replication of McClelland-Winterbottom studies. *Dissertation Abstracts International, 35*, 593A. (University Microfilms No. 74-14, 942)

Zaccaro, S. J. (1984). The role of task attractiveness. *Personality and Social Psychology Bulletin, 10*, 99–106.

Zajonc, R. (1985). Cognitive theories in social psychology. In G. Lindzey & E. Aronson (Eds.), *Handbook of social psychology* (Vol. 1) (pp. 320–411). New York: Random House.

Index